Journey into Community:

Looking Inside the Community Learning Center

Steve R. Parson

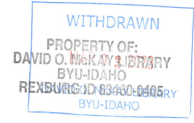

EYE ON EDUCATION
6 DEPOT WAY WEST, SUITE 106
LARCHMONT, NY 10538
(914) 833–0551
(914) 833–0761 fax
www.eyeoneducation.com

Library of Congress Cataloging-in-Publication Data

Parson, Steve R.
    Journey into community : looking inside the community learning center / Steve R. Parson.
        p. cm.
    ISBN 1-930556-67-5
    1. Community schools--United States. 2. Community and school--United States. 3. School improvement programs--United States. I. Title.

LB2820.P35 2004
371.19--dc22   2003060185

10 9 8 7 6 5 4 3 2 1

Editorial and production services provided by
Richard H. Adin Freelance Editorial Services
52 Oakwood Blvd., Poughkeepsie, NY 12603-4112
(914-471-3566)

Also Available
from EYE ON EDUCATION

**Transforming Schools
into Community Learning Centers**
Steve R. Parson

**Achievement Now!
How to Assure No Child is Left Behind**
Dr. Donald J. Fielder

**Strategies to Help Solve
Our School Dropout Problem**
Franklin P. Schargel and Jay Smink

Dropout Prevention Tools
Franklin P. Schargel

**Student Transitions from Middle to High School:
Improving Achievement and Creating a Safer
Environment**
J. Allen Queen

**Constructivist Strategies:
Meeting Standards and Engaging Adolescent Minds**
Foote, Vermette, and Battaglia

The Directory of Programs for Students at Risk
Thomas Williams

Dealing with Difficult Parents (And with Parents in Difficult Situations)
Whitaker and Fiore

**101 "Answers" for New Teachers and Their Mentors:
Effective Teaching Tips for Daily Classroom Use**
Annette L. Breaux

**Motivating and Inspiring Teachers:
The Educational Leader's Guide
for Building Staff Morale**
Todd Whitaker, Beth Whitaker, and Dale Lumpa

About the Author

Steve Parson has spent his entire professional career as an advocate for the concept of community education. He has served as president of the National Community Education Association and is a member of the 21st Century Community Learning Centers Training Task Force. At Virginia Tech he has served as an associate dean, department head, director of a graduate center and a faculty member in the Educational Leadership program. He frequently serves as a speaker and consultant for school communities involved in developing Community Learning Centers.

Steve is also involved in providing support to schools that have implemented the Basic School Model developed by Ernest Boyer. He serves as the co-director of The Basic School Network—Eastern Consortia.

Prior to the publication of this book he authored *Transforming Schools into Community Learning Centers*. Steve lives with his wife Marolyn in Alexandria, Virginia.

Acknowledgements

This book would not have been possible without the involvement of, and input from many of the graduate students that have been enrolled in our Educational Leadership graduate programs at Virginia Tech. Students reviewed manuscript chapters for both writing style and content. They often asked excellent questions that would send me back to the drawing board. They also shared numerous examples of things they were doing in their schools to connect with families and communities.

I am also indebted to my colleagues in the Community Education movement who have been a great support system for my work throughout my career. Support from the Charles S. Mott Foundation provided my doctoral program fellowship as well as grants that provided resources for many of the projects I have undertaken over the years.

The cover photo was taken by Dick Dillon. I also wish to thank Brian M. Hoffer of the Milwaukee Public Schools' Department of Recreation and Community Services for his assistance with the cover photo.

Last, but not least I need to recognize someone very special in my personal and professional life. My wife Marolyn Parson has shared the high points and low points over more years that she will allow me to mention. Thanks to all of you.

Foreword

Yogi Berra once said, "When you come to a fork in the road, take it." Unfortunately, not every path will take us on the journey we necessarily want. Steve's book, fortunately, provides us a roadmap, a journey into improvements in community and education—through win–win partnerships.

Transforming a school into a Community Learning Center is a powerful approach to better schools, better communities, and better learning for students of all ages. It is a 21st-century solution. Community Learning Centers are an educational concept and an on-the-ground approach to better education from Mongolia to Brazil.

Yet, in American education, we seem to enjoy entering into one philosophical battle after another—no wonder we have had difficulty as a nation moving with a sustained effort to improve schools and education. We have had the *reading wars*—phonetics versus whole-language. The *math wars* are still brewing, and so on, and so forth.

Transforming schools into Community Learning Centers is a rare strategy that cuts across most philosophical persuasions. Steve captures it in clear examples and down-to-earth descriptions of how critical features of successful schools and parent and community connections can be powerful in improving learning and communities.

Although the concept of a Community Learning Center is very inviting, it often seems to those fighting the daily battles in education to be removed from the *real* work of teachers, principals, school reformers, parent and community leaders, and policy makers. The chapters in this book make the Community Learning Center come alive and make it become a real asset in education improvement and in the real work of educators and community leaders.

We want greater accountability, we want our students to achieve higher standards, we want greater parent and family involvement, we want the extra time and extra connections available through quality after school programs, we want our students and families to acquire the technological skills to be equipped for this century, we want to utilize the vibrant learning resources in our communities, and we want our teachers and principals to have all the tools they need to be successful. We often tackle these issues in isolation, and as a result we are often frustrated and unsuccessful.

Journey into Community gives educators, parents, and community leaders the concrete tools to address these many important and related issues in education today. Turning a school and its partners into a Community Learning Center and partnership is not a panacea for all of education's ills and opportunities, but it provides a solid foundation and general approach to doing business—the people's business of constantly improving public education.

As Steve was writing this terrific book, the United States was going through one of the most challenging times in terms of public funding of education and other public services. It was not uncommon to hear of schools, colleges, and children's services being cut by 10 to 20 percent. The initial reactions, as has happened before in these times of budget crises, is to cut back and eliminate the very tools to help children with the greatest needs to keep up and catch up. Extended learning opportunities, school–community partnerships, extracurricular activities, the arts, tutoring and mentoring, and family outreach, among many other aspects of improving learning opportunities, were being considered for major cutbacks or even elimination.

These added budget challenges should not be looked on as an excuse to turn away from schools as Community Learning Centers, but rather as a greater incentive to move toward them. We know that it will take extra time, extra help, extra hands, extra opportunities, and new partnerships to be successful. Steve's book gives us an important framework and set of actions toward that success, regardless of the current budget climate.

Terry Peterson

Dr. Terry Peterson is the director of the Afterschool National Resource Network. He also holds the position of Senior Fellow for Policy and Partnerships at the University of South Carolina and at the College of Charleston. Dr. Peterson served as the chief education advisor to the United States Secretary of Education for eight years.

Table of Contents

Introducing
the Journey into
Community

This book is about a journey. That journey begins when a traditional school decides to end the isolation from its community. William Carr's (1942) writing about schools being separated from the community by a moat, and of drawbridges being lowered so the children of the mainland can go out to the island to learn to live on the mainland, sets the context for this book. We still see remnants of those moats and drawbridges in schools across the land. The moats today may not be as deep or as wide, but they still exist.

The Community Learning Center is all about education making a journey into the community and the community making the journey into the school. We all have a lot to gain by these trips. We can use the Community Learning Center as a key to unlock vast storehouse of resources in the community that can support the important task of educating our youth. We can also unlock the resources within the center to make them available to enrich the lives of all the citizens of the community.

Since the publication of *Transforming Schools into Community Learning Centers,* I have often been asked for more detail on how teaching and learning would change when a school becomes a Community Learning Center. While I didn't intend to slight teaching and learning, it was true that I hadn't spent much time providing texture and detail to that aspect of the Community Learning Center.

With this book I have focused on how teaching and learning can be transformed to match the vision of the Community Learning Center. There are many dimensions of teaching and learning that will be addressed as I take you on a journey through a Community Learning Center, to look over the shoulder of teachers and students as they work together in this new learning environment. Each chapter will begin with a scenario describing life in the Community Learning Center. Those scenarios illustrate the changing relationship between the centers and the communities they serve.

You will see teachers providing leadership in ways that raises the level of professional commitment to quality education for students. Visible through out the book will be community resources supporting academic success for all students, not just a special few. Partnerships will also be seen as an important part of the new landscape. These partnerships among teachers and families, schools and communities, and providers of services to families are all aimed at helping students to be successful in achieving at high academic levels.

The school day in the Community Learning Center will continue to be lively long after most traditional schools have sent their buses on their way delivering children to their homes—homes that often lack adult supervision until the early evening hours. You will see how afterschool programs are being connected to regular-day program in ways that support student learning and provide opportunities for enrichment activities in a safe environment. Teaching and learning time is further extended in the Community Learning Center through the extended-year calendar. Where traditional schools use 180 days (and sometimes even less) for instruction, the Community Learning Centers use a 220–230 day schedule.

Community Learning Centers have been created in a standards-based environment, with teachers feeling pressure to provide students the greatest chance for success. Elements in the Community Learning Center are working together to con-tribute to that success.

The unusual sight of agencies and organizations that serve children and families working together will emerge on our journey. Turf wars will not be visible because the high level of collaboration will have eliminated them. Obsolete will be the sense of disenfranchisement that is often seen in teachers, stu-dents, and parents who have been left out of the decision mak-ing process in traditional schools. Shared decision making in the Community Learning Center provides a new sense of ownership and inclusion.

We will also see technology being integrated into the teaching in ways that we have not seen in schools in the past. And no visit to a school would be complete with out a stop in the principal's office. The title on the door may well be some-thing other than "principal," but we will see what the role of leadership in the Community Learning Center looks like.

The ideas and concepts for the Community Learning Cen-ter that are presented in this book represent a composite of the many great innovations that are being seen in community schools across the country. There has been a deliberate at-tempt to not limit the Community Learning Center vision to an elementary or a secondary model. The concept of the Com-munity Learning Center can be adapted first to the needs of the community and then to the resources available to address those needs regardless of the age of the children and youth who are enrolled.

I hope that the ideas and examples presented inside the covers of this book will provide inspiration for schools and communities to continue to plan for the transition of their schools to Community Learning Centers. Each of these cen-ters will take on their own particular look, shape, and form, as a product of the needs of the communities they serve and the resources available in that community. I hope that your jour-ney through this book is both enlightening and reinforcing. For many of you, much of what you read will reinforce things you already believe in and are doing in your schools. I hope that there will also be those things in the book that you will find to cause you to stop and think, "Wow, that is an idea I had not thought of before."

If, in your journey, you come across things that you would like to share with other fellow travelers, or things that puzzle you, I encourage you to send them on to me. For the puzzles, I may be able to connect you with someone who has dealt with that problem before, but I make no promises for solutions to all your problems. I can be reached best through email at parson@vt.edu.

Thanks for joining me on this important journey.

References

Carr, W. (1942). *Community life in a democracy.* Chicago: National Association of Parents and Teachers.

1

Schools Becoming Community Learning Centers

Journey into Community

The building housing the Community Learning Center has a very different feel from the minute you walk in the front door. Instead of warning signs telling the public to report to the office immediately, there are signs that say, "Welcome. We are glad you are here. Please visit the office where we can help you find your way." When we arrive at the office, we see that the front counter is gone, and we find instead a warm and open environment with comfortable chairs for those who need to wait.

There is a steady flow of adults from the community and students from a nearby college who are signing in as volunteers. They have come to provide a wide variety of help, ranging from the traditional teacher-assistant volunteers to mentors for students who need caring and supportive adults in their lives.

Down the hall is the Family Resource Center, where parents go to find out more about how their children are doing in school, get information about resources available to parents and families, and access a computer that can provide with a wide range of information about the Community Learning Center. They can also use the computer for word-processing tasks like preparing a job resume, or they can access the center's website to find out what programs and services are offered in the center for parents and other community members.

One of the center's business partners is using the gym for a wellness activity for their employees. Some adults and high school seniors are in one of the classrooms, where they are taking an evening college credit course offered by the local community college. The high school students will be able to earn dual credit and use the course to speed up their college education. The adults save having to drive 45 miles each way to attend the course on the main campus.

Why Change?

Everywhere we turn, there are voices calling for schools to change. This is not something new, but the volume of the conversation has definitely been turned way up. The problem is that there is no clear consensus about what those *changed schools* should look like. Many people use the term *reform* when talking about this change in schools. Personally, I am not always comfortable with the use of reform in connection with education. In the impressively thick *The American Heritage Dictionary* (2000, p. 1468), which my former textbook consultant sister gave me one Christmas, there are several options for defining *reform*.

The first definition is, "To improve by alteration, correction of error, or removal of defects; put into a better condition." That works pretty well for me. It is the second and third options that I have problems with: "2a. To abolish abuse or malpractice," "2b. To put an end to a wrong," and my favorite, "3. To cause (a person) to give up harmful or immoral practices."

I cannot accept the idea that all our schools have been subject to abuse, malpractice, or wrongdoing. Yes, they are in desperate need of improvement, but that need for improvement comes from years of taking public education for granted. Some would have us believe that we have seen astronomical increases in tax dollars to support public schools. If that were true, I would ask, "Why is it that teachers are still earning salaries that are not competitive enough to attract and retain the numbers of qualified individuals needed to fill our nation's classrooms?" "Why are many of our children, especially in our urban and rural communities, attending school in buildings that are outdated and unsafe?"

The well-known educator, John Dewey (1897, p. 79), once wrote,

> I believe that it is the business of every one interested in education to insist upon the school as the primary and most effective interest of social progress and reform in order that society may be awakened to realize what the school stands for, and

aroused to the necessity of endowing the educator with the sufficient equipment properly to perform his task.

Our communities must be engaged in the Community Learning Center to mobilize the resources that are needed to recognize that the education is critical to social progress.

At the root of change is the need to link our schools more closely to the communities they serve. There are several reasons that make this change important to the future of our children.

- ◆ Education needs to become a top priority for all members of the community.
- ◆ All the resources of the community need to be engaged to meet the needs of our children.
- ◆ Every member of the community needs to develop a sense of ownership of the Community Learning Centers serving them.
- ◆ The resources of the Community Learning Center need to serve all the residents of the community.

In the chapters that follow I will attempt to provide a pathway for schools as they make the journey from a traditional school to Community Learning Center.

What's in it for Kids and Communities?

The important issue in changing our schools is what these changes will do for our kids and our communities. When our kids see education becoming a community focus, when they see their parents engaged in their education, and when they see other members of the community take an active interest in education, that is when the Community Learning Center begins to have a real impact on kids and their academic success.

Communities gain when schools become Community Learning Centers that are open to serving the entire community. This doesn't mean that the resources that are needed to education children are diluted. It means that we can maximize our resources by creating greater collaboration among the school, the community, and the agencies that serve families.

What Is the Potential Outcome for Kids and Communities?

In the field of partnership development we have learned that it is important to consider the WIIFM—"What's In It For Me"—in every relationship. This is based on the reality that individuals and groups are motivated by what they will gain from a relationship or action. The same is true about the development of a Community Learning Center. The box that follows contains some potential WIIFMs that can help drive the transformation of schools into Community Learning Centers.

What's In It For Me?

Kids—Children of all ages in the community will gain a safe and secure environment where they can grow and develop all day and all year. They have a community that is truly dedicated to supporting learning for all students. They have a voice in deciding their future. They are respected and nurtured by a multitude of others.

Educators—Educators feel that they are appreciated partners with the community in the important task of providing for the educational and developmental needs of those who live in the community. Resources from the community support them in helping students achieve at high levels. Educators also gain much-needed support from the community, which is important in maintaining a tax base that will furnish the resources needed to provide quality education throughout the community.

Parents and Community Members—They share in the accountability for learning in the community. They also gain a voice in how the resources of the community can be best used to support the learning that needs to take place in the Community Learning Center. They gain access to valuable resources that are located in Community Learning Centers in the form of computer centers, libraries, and recreation and wellness facilities, as well as teachers who are dedicated to creating a learning environment that supports learning for all. They also get support for the important task of parenting.

Community- and Family-Serving Agencies—Agencies in the community that serve families and children gain access to resources through a process of collaboration that is fostered through the Community Learning Center. This collaboration often never existed before the development of the Community Learning Center. Agencies were left to scrap among themselves for resources that were viewed as scarce and inadequate to meet the towering list of needs that they were being expected to meet.

Business Leaders—The Community Learning Center works hard at establishing partnerships with businesses and other community groups. Businesses benefit by having a larger pool of qualified individuals to choose from for the level of staff needed to run a profitable business. Business leaders are given the opportunity to be at the table when decisions are made about how students are being prepared to enter the future workforce. Businesses are also presented with opportunities to demonstrate that they do care about the community and want to be good citizens, as they contribute to improving the quality of education and community life.

Definition of Community Learning Centers

The best way to define a Community Learning Center might be to look at how one community has chosen to shape their centers. The example here is in Milwaukee, Wisconsin, but it could have been drawn from any of the hundreds of communities that have developed Community Learning Centers over the past few years.

Milwaukee Community Learning Centers' Mission

Milwaukee Public Schools' 21st Century Community Learning Centers (CLCs) help strengthen families, reduce crime, and improve neighborhoods. Open after school, evenings, and weekends and during the summer, the CLCs are committed to learning, enrichment and support activities that help lessen exposure to negative influences. Ultimately, a CLC builds a strong neighborhood and makes our community a better place to live.

Vision

Our vision is to unite 100 MPS schools with community organizations, businesses, government, agencies, families and neighborhood residents to encourage academic achievement and strengthen neighborhoods. CLCs and neighborhood schools go hand in hand to provide a support system that focuses on positive youth, family and neighborhood development. The 21st Century Community Learning Centers are staffed by caring adults from youth-serving agencies, schools and the community. Their commitment is to provide a healthy balance of learning and fun in a safe and supportive environment. Young people will have additional hours to learn, which helps increase academic achievement, attendance and graduation rates. Both young people and adults will have more opportunities to develop skills to help them achieve personal success. (Milwaukee Public Schools, 2001, p. 2)

It should be noted that the Milwaukee Public Schools are located at the center of one of the nation's most aggressive experiments in school choice. Parents in the city have the ability to make a choice about where their children attend school (including private schools). The public schools have made the decision to use the Community Learning Center concept to make the schools more attractive to students and their families.

Teacher's Role in the Transition

Teachers play a key role in transforming a traditional school into a Community Learning Center. The decision to examine the Community Learning Center as a model for change can happen as a result of teacher leadership in the school and community. They serve as members of teams who travel to visit successful Community Learning Centers in other communities. They establish linkages with teachers in those Community Learning Centers to learn more about how the teaching and learning process differs from the traditional schools.

Teachers have often been part of writing teams that have developed grant applications to seek funding for creating Community Learning Centers under the U.S. Department of Education's 21st Century Community Learning Centers grant program. Teachers also serve as members of steering councils that are charged with the task of guiding the transformation process from traditional school to Community Learning Center. Their participation in the transition process ensures that the teaching and learning processes will be given careful consideration as the transition is made. Teachers can also help in identifying students and parents to serve on the steering council and in other leadership roles in the Community Learning Center.

Common Components
in Community Learning Centers

A Community Learning Center can be developed from a traditional school, in a traditional school building, in any community. It can also be built from the ground up, as we find in the case of brand-new schools or charter schools. There are several components that will be found in common regardless of where the journey began.

Community resources become a regular part of the instructional program.

The buildings stay open later and are often used by the community when not needed for classroom activities.

Numerous partnerships between the center and the community provide an exchange of resources that are of value to all members of the partnerships. These partnerships also contribute support to student academic achievement.

Services are provided to whole community in addition to focusing on the educational needs of children.

Community agencies servicing families and children work together in the Community Learning Center to provide needed programs and services.

The center provides a place where people throughout the community can access technology.

Families are actively engaged in the education of their children.

The school day is extended through afterschool programs that provide kids a safe place to go where they receive academic and personal enrichment.

Leadership is shared among all of the community stakeholders.

Changing the Culture

One of the most critical changes that will take place when a traditional school makes a transition to a Community Learning Center is the change that takes place in the culture. It might be a good time to note that many of the new models of Community Learning Centers are showing up in newly formed charter schools. The reason for this is that building a new school from the ground up allows the builders to establish a new culture from the very beginning. This is much easier than to change a culture that has taken years to develop.

The time that change takes place is also a factor in the transformation to Community Learning Centers. Most experts in educational change tell us that minor adjustments take a minimum of three to five years to become effective, and major changes take five to seven years to become established.

Traditional schools tend to be characterized by some of the following cultural characteristics.

Traditional School Culture

- ◆ Teachers are isolated by classroom, discipline, and grade level.
- ◆ Parent and family involvement is channeled into teacher conferences, open-house programs, and parent-teacher associations (with maybe a band or athletic booster club mixed in at the secondary level).
- ◆ Contracts for teachers offer employment only during the academic year, with layoffs in the summer months.
- ◆ Few community resources are involved in supporting classroom instruction.
- ◆ Community partnerships are limited to "adopt-a-school" models.

Community Learning Center Culture

The Community Learning Center culture takes on a very different look when compared to the traditional school.

- ◆ Teachers work in teams and collaborate across disciplines and grade levels.

- ◆ Parents and families are engaged as partners in their children's learning.

- ◆ Community Learning Centers operate on an extended-year schedule in which teachers are offered full employment and salaries that are competitive with other professions with similar qualification.

- ◆ Mentors, tutors, instructional materials, and even some instructors from the community are integrated into the instructional process to enrich the resource base dedicated to improving student success.

- ◆ Community partnerships in the Community Learning Center feature good planning and implementation, and they keep track of the impact of partnership activities on student achievement.

As you continue to read this book, you will find many more ways that the Community Learning Center is different from the traditional school. Many of these differences come in ways that you may not have previously thought of.

Recently, a student in one of my classes read *Transforming Schools into Community Learning Center* (Parson, 1999) while he was completing an administrative internship in Kipps Elementary School in Blacksburg, Virginia. This was a newly opened school with a new principal, faculty, and building. The leaders of that school have used many of the concepts found in the Community Learning Center model, along with the ideas of Ernest Boyer's (1994) Basic School model. The student did an analysis comparing Kipps to a traditional model and a Community Learning Center. As you can see from the chart on the next page, Kipps has produced a close approximation of a Community Learning Center.

Figure 1.1. Transforming Schools into Community Learning Centers

Comparing the Traditional School with the Community Learning Center and with Kipps Elementary School (Bezzell, 1999)

Criteria	Traditional School	Community Learning Center
Time	5 days a week 6–8 hours a day 180–200 days a year 50-minute class periods	7 days a week 10–12 hours a day 300+ days a year Extended blocks of time

Kipps Elementary School (KES)
7 days a week (parks & rec programs inc.)
12+ hours a day (Adventure Club before and after school; whole school and individual class activities frequently extend into evening hours)
300+ days a year (6-week summer program plus parks and rec, 4-H, et al.)
Time blocks are flexible to meet instructional needs.

Space	Education takes place in a classroom.	Education takes place throughout the community.

KES
Education takes place throughout the local and broader community, including Virginia Tech and Radford University cultural programs and field trips to the fire department, the bank, retirement homes and hospitals, Williamsburg, and Gettysburg.

Relationships to other agencies and organizations	Few connections with other agencies and organizations.	Collaboration with other community agencies to provide services to families and children.

KES

Adventure Club offers before- and afterschool programs from 6 A.M. to 6 P.M. The parks and rec department offers free play and structured programs in the gym (built collaboratively with the school) and activity fields. Virginia Tech and Radford University students use the school as a laboratory to develop their skills while contributing their unique talents to the students and staff. Partnerships are established with community businesses and organizations that participate in school activities.

Family and Community Involvement	Involvement limited to parent participation in such activities as open houses and parent conferences.	A comprehensive process of community involvement in a wide range of programs and activities.

KES

Parents and community members are in the school daily serving in a variety of capacities, including office and classroom volunteers, PTA members, helpers with site-based management activities, and substitute teachers. A bus is sent to neighborhoods to encourage participation in evening PTA programs, which occur at least monthly. Parent conferences are scheduled for mornings, afternoons, or evenings at the parents' convenience.

Instruction	One teacher lectures to a homogeneous group of students. Emphasis is on paper-and-pencil, norm-referenced tests. Instruction is limited to resources represented by the teacher and the textbooks. Students focus on individual assignments.	Teams of teachers work with groups of students of varying abilities. Authentic assessment is used to test whether students can use their knowledge in real-world situations.

KES

Students and teachers are grouped in a variety of ways for instructional purposes. Special-needs students are fully in- cluded, unless it is in the *student's* best interest to be pulled out for instruction. Some teachers team with another teacher extensively. Multigrade grouping is done through partner- ing one class with another and creating "families" of one class each from grades K–5. Cooperative learning and au- thentic assessment are used extensively. Local experts from the community are used as resources.

| Use of Technology | Instructional technology is centered in the media center and computer labs. Technology hardware is reserved for student use only—and only during the regular school day. A few specialists are trained to use instructional technology. There is little access to telecommunications resources such as the Internet. Except for videotapes, televised instruction is not part of the school's program. | Instructional technology is located throughout the school. Technology hardware is available for student, family, and community use. All teachers, staff, and students have the skills to use multimedia technology. Networks give all classrooms access to the Internet. Interactive, two-way–televised instruction is used to enrich offerings for all students and the community. |

KES

Each classroom at Kipps is networked to the Internet and to a library server providing a wide variety of instructional software choices. Each classroom has a television with cable hookup and a VCR. Staff uses software for instruction, staff development, and community presentations.

Leadership	Decisions are made by central office staff or by principals. Principals are expected to be leaders for their schools and are held accountable for results. Parents and community have no voice in developing plans for the school or deciding how resources will be used.	Decision making is a shared responsibility of principals, teachers, staff, parents, students, and members of the school community. Leadership is shared among all stakeholders in the school community, who are held jointly accountable for results. Parents and the community have multiple opportunities to be involved in developing an annual plan and deciding how resources are to be used.

KES

Parents, teachers, and staff have multiple opportunities to share in decision making and are encouraged to do so. The site-based–management team includes teachers from each grade level, a specialty area representative, a special education representative, a paraprofessional representative, parent representatives from each grade level, a PTA representative, and a community member who does not have children at Kipps. A teacher-led staff-development committee determines needs and plans staff development accordingly. A team of grade-level representatives brings grade-level concerns to administration.

It is no coincidence that schools that have implemented Boyer's Basic School model have many elements in common with the Community Learning Centers described in this book. Ernest Boyer was a strong influence on the thinking that has gone into this work. For more on the Basic School model at Kipps Elementary, you can access two doctoral dissertations the feature studies of that school. The website for Virginia Tech's electronic dissertation collection is http://scholar.lib.vt.edu/theses/. The students to look for are Patricia Talbot ("Critical Beginnings: Creating School Community for All Children and Families") and Ray Van Dyke ("A Case Study of the Implementation of Ernest Boyer's Basic School Framework School").

Extended School Year

Before we leave this examination of what changes when a traditional school becomes a Community Learning Center, we need to take a look at the resource of time. Later we will be looking at how afterschool programs are used to extend the school day. In addition, Community Learning Centers also extend the school year.

Most schools in this country have stuck by the sacred 180-day calendar. At the same time, we are faced with our students being compared to those of countries around the world who have 210–235 days of instruction. There is a year-round school movement in this country that has attracted a lot of attention in recent years. However, most of the schools that have become part of that movement have used a calendar that takes the same 180 days and distributes them more evenly over the year. This does potentially help prevent the learning drop-off experienced by some students during the long summer break. But for most schools it does not add additional time for teaching and learning to take place.

We have to remind ourselves that most school calendars are still influenced by an agricultural economy that we have long left behind. Students had to help with the work on family farms during the summer, and school calendars were set to accommodate that need. Children no longer need to work in the fields in the summer, unless you consider the employment needs of amusement parks. In Virginia we have what is commonly referred to as the "King's Dominion" rule, where schools are not allowed to begin classes before Labor Day. King's Dominion is a large amusement park located just north of Richmond that depends heavily on school-age youth employees and customers.

An important fact to keep in mind when considering the amount of instructional time provided in the Community Learning Center is that all children can learn, but some take longer than others. The extended-year calendar provides for those students who need more time to learn what they need to meet the new high standards that have been set for them. We have seen in many school districts across the country a sort of creeping year-round school movement. Although they have no formal year-round calendar, the enrollments in summer school have been doubling and tripling every year for the past four or five years. The need for students to have more instruction to meet state testing standards has caused the bulge in enrollments. Some communities are now enrolling 60 to 70 percent of their students in summer school programs. The Community Learning Center has taken all these issues into consideration when adopting an extended year calendar. This allows for instruction to be planned in a more comprehensive manner, rather than having to approach it in blocks that would include summer school.

Before we leave this focus on the extended-year calendar, we need to recognize some of the issues that accompany the shift from a traditional calendar. First, some teachers will oppose the extended year. One of the main objections is that they were attracted to teaching so they could have the summer off to spend time with their children. Although that is a nice feature of employment as a teacher, the truth is that many teachers wind up having to seek summer employment to earn enough income to provide for their families. With the extended school year we are able to employ teachers for 12 months, rather then the present 9½ or 10 months. The result is that their pay increases proportionally, and we wind up with annual salaries that are more comparable to those in other fields with similar academic preparation. John Grisham (1995, p.143), the popular novelist, once wrote, "If lawyers earned the same salaries as school teachers, they'd immediately close nine law schools out of ten."

Family vacations become the other issue when extending the calendar. With an extended school year we can schedule more breaks at different times of the year. Family vacations can be scheduled throughout the year, thus accommodating the many families who prefer times other than summer for their vacations.

The journey to a Community Learning Center is not an easy one, nor is it one that will be quickly completed. Change cannot take place overnight in the process of transforming a traditional school. It is not a journey that can be undertaken alone. The travelers must include a wide range of stakeholders from the community who are committed to improving the quality of education. The circle of involvement must be enlarged as the journey progresses until the point where the whole community is engaged.

References

The American heritage dictionary (2000). New York: Houghton Mifflin.

Bezzell, B. (1999). *Comparing the traditional school with the community learning center and with Kipps Elementary School.* Unpublished paper.

Boyer, E. (1994). *The Basic School: A community for learning.* Princeton, NJ: The Carnegie Foundation for the Advancement of Teaching.

Dewey, J. (1897, January). My pedagogic creed. *The School Journal, LIV*(3).

Grisham, J. (1995). *The Rainmaker.* New York: Doubleday.

Milwaukee Public Schools (2001). *21st century community learning centers.* Author.

Parson, S. R. (1999). *Transforming schools into community learning centers.* Larchmont, NY: Eye on Education.

Talbot, P. (1998). Critical beginnings: Creating school community for all children and families. Unpublished dissertation, Virginia Polytechnic Institute & State University: Blacksburg, VA.

Van Dyke, R.E. (1998). A case study of the implementation of Ernest Boyer's basic school framework in one elementary school. Unpublished dissertation, Blacksburg, VA.

2

The Changing View of Teaching

Journey into Community

As you travel down the halls and look into classrooms, you will find few examples of neat rows of desks lined up. You will find rooms organized to allow for more student interaction in groups, more space for students to actually work, and lots of student access to networked computer workstations. You will see less "teacher talk" and more instruction where students are being guided to seek knowledge and understanding from work that they perform. That work may be problem solving, it may be some original research, or it may involve using resources from the community to understand how knowledge is applied in the real world.

Teachers can often be seen meeting with other teachers to plan collaborative teaching activities, coordinate joint curricular initiatives, and discuss how various approaches to teaching are working or not working. Teachers are involved in studying their own practice through action research projects. And they are not afraid to say that what they are doing is not working and move on to try another approach.

Teachers are actively involved in building community, within both the school and the community served by the center. They are especially visible in working to establish partnerships with the parents of their students. They understand the positive connection that research has made between engaging the student's families and the academic success experienced by students. Parents are treated as valued partners in the education of their children, and there is a comprehensive plan that involves multiple research-based strategies to engage all the families, not just a small percentage.

Teaching has changed considerably since most of us were students. We have seen the learning styles *research* that tell us that kids learn in a variety of ways and that each individual learner has his or her own specific learning pattern. Howard Gardner's (1999) work in defining the multiple intelligence that students bring with them into the classroom, and the work of Rita and Kenneth Dunn (http://arapaho.nsuok.edu/~oil/) at their Oklahoma Institute for Learning Styles, have given teachers tools to begin to address individual student differences as they design curriculum and learning activities in their classrooms.

One of my students, Andrea Bengier, studied a team of middle school teachers working together to improve their instruction. Those teachers were committed to using information about individual students as they planned their instructional strategies. Bengier (2000, p. 73) observed, "The teachers reflected on what they had learned about their students and made sure that they were including the learning style preferences of the students in assignments. The teachers often offered choices in the student assignments based on learning style varieties".

The movement toward constructivism has also begun to have an impact on the way teachers teach. In the past we saw the teacher as the "distributor of knowledge." This role was sometimes characterized as the "sage on the stage." In a constructivist classroom, however, the teacher is more accurately described as the "guide on the side." This means a change from lecture and worksheets to a style of teaching that puts teachers in the position of facilitating learning for students as they become actively involved in creating their own knowledge.

At the beginning of the 1990s researcher Linda Darling-Hammond (1993, p. 754) described the teacher's job as no longer being to "cover the curriculum," but to empower learners to develop their individual talents. Darling-Hammond described how teachers use constructivism to reach curriculum goals:

> To foster meaningful learning, teachers must construct experiences that allow students to confront powerful ideas whole. They must create bridges

between the very different experiences of individual learners and the common curriculum goals. They must use a variety of approaches to build on the conceptions, cultures, interests, motivations, and learning modes of their students. They must understand how their students think as well as what they know.

Teachers are now able to focus on teaching ideas and concepts rather than getting through all the chapters in the textbook by the end of the year. Textbooks become resources supporting learning instead of being the sole focus of learning. Rather than "drill and kill" exercises, teachers are beginning to guide student learning by using problems that are relevant to the students. They are centering their teaching on primary concepts and essential questions that are the focus of active learning on the part of students.

John Dewey and his progressive education movement represented one of the first voices advocating students as active participants in their own learning, rather than passive recipients of knowledge that was "poured into them" by teachers. In the essay, "My Pedagogic Creed," Dewey (1897, p. 34) made his belief in the role of the learner very clear:

> I believe that much of present education fails because it neglects this fundamental principle of the school as a form of community life. It conceives the school as a place where certain information is to be given, where certain lessons are to be learned, or where certain habits are to be formed. The value of these is conceived as lying largely in the remote future; the child must do these things for the sake of something else he is to do; they are mere preparation. As a result they do not become a part of the life experience of the child and are not truly educative.

Teaching as the Loneliest Job

Teaching has often been described as one of the loneliest jobs anyone can have. That loneliness has come from the isolation of classrooms. Teachers have been captives of classrooms and a pattern of teaching that calls for one teacher to be responsible for the learning of 20 to 30+ students in one classroom, depending on how well the school district has done in reducing class size. This practice of isolation has created many problems for teachers.

- ◆ Few opportunities to observe the teaching of others

- ◆ Little opportunity to obtain feedback on their own teaching

- ◆ Lack of opportunity to share what they know about the learning styles of individual students

- ◆ Curriculum that artificially segments learning and denies the ability to integrate subject matter

- ◆ No convenient times and places to have professional dialogue about common teaching experiences

- ◆ Little time to contact families about the progress being made by their students

This isolation has often been identified as one of the primary causes of teachers leaving the profession after just one or two years. For the new teachers who do stick it out, those first few years are often a struggle that takes place alone in their classrooms without much help from their colleagues.

Team Teaching

At one point in my own teaching career at the university I got roped into a team-teaching experience that completely changed the way I viewed the teaching and learning process. I had just decided to end a six-year stint in administration in the university to return to what I like to do most, teach. A couple of friends on our faculty, knowing that I was returning to teaching, approached me with an offer I could not refuse. "Was I interested in joining a group of faculty who were going to be designing a new doctoral program?" This new program would involve a faculty team who would stay with a cohort of students until they completed their program of studies. The program would enroll both classroom teachers and school administrators, and it would feature a curriculum that would focus on leadership, inquiry, and change.

Without boring the reader with extensive details about the grand time we had working together, let me offer a brief summary of what the experience provided to the faculty who were part of the team.

- Teaching was fun because we had a team that enjoyed working together.
- We were able to draw on the distinct talents and expertise of every member of the team.
- Students could choose among team members for one-on-one advice and assistance.
- The time spent together in planning provided a focused approach to our instruction.
- We were able to share our individual views of each student's progress.
- We all had many opportunities to become learners in the program, as well as teachers.
- We were able to support one another in trying new approaches to instruction and program design that we might not have tried alone.
- This particular student cohort experienced a nearly 90-percent rate of degree completion.

I have just described what happened in a university teaching environment, and although the conditions in working with adult doctoral students may not always have much in common with teaching adolescents or young children, there is some definite commonality in the potential relationships among faculty.

It needs to be said that not all teachers will immediately be drawn to an opportunity to become part of a teaching team. One experience I had recently with a teaching team illustrates one aspect of that reluctance to teaming. A colleague and I, who had teamed together on several occasions, were meeting with a new member of our faculty who had been assigned to work with us in planning instruction for a cohort of students who were preparing to become principals. At our first meeting, after about an hour of conversation about what it was we were going to teach and some instructional approaches we might use, the new member of the faculty blurted out, "You guys are really serious about this team thing!" She said that it was suddenly obvious that we were indeed proposing to function as a team, with everyone making a contribution to the task. She said that her only previous experience with teaching teams was more like "turn teaching." When they got together to plan, it was a matter of, "You do this on these dates, and I will do that on those dates."

Our approach to teaming involved the creative process of the members of the team pooling their ideas and experiences to plan and deliver the instruction. We all had ownership of the whole process, not just our little piece of the whole. We were able to capitalize on the concept of synergism; that is, the sum of the parts had greater energy when working together than when each of us acted independently.

After my experiences over the past dozen years of being part of some highly effective teams, it is extremely difficult to walk into a classroom by myself. It is not out of doubt about my own ability to teach a particular course, but it is in knowing that I am going to be limited in the creative assets that I alone bring to the class.

Over the past decade the nation's middle schools have been experimenting with interdisciplinary teaching teams and team grouping of students. Those teams of teachers have produced some remarkable results. Wheelock (2000, p. 2), writing in the newsletter of the Turning Points Project, *Conversations*, described what is taking place in these schools:

> In middle schools around the country, teachers collaborate informally all the time. Some use morning sign-in routines to check on details for a field trip. Others use their lunch break to arrange for one-time classroom activities with a specialist. Teachers in Turning Points schools go the next step, building on these interactions to establish more formal modes of professional collaboration directed to improving teaching and learning.

There are many lessons that can be learned from the Turning Points experience that fit into the design of the Community Learning Center. The principles presented in the following box have been used to guide the work of educators in promoting the intellectual, social, and personal accomplishments of their students.

Turning Points Core Principles

- Create small caring communities for learning.
- Teach a core academic program based on rigorous standards.
- Ensure success for all students.
- Empower teachers and administrators to make decisions.
- Staff the middle grades with teachers who are expert at teaching young adolescents.
- Create an environment that supports a healthy, enriching lifestyle that develops students' character, creativity, health, and fitness.
- Engage families in the education of young adolescents.
- Connect schools and communities to enable students to engage in learning, service and citizenship.

Source: Center for Collaborative Education, 2000

If we exclude the use of the terms *middle grades* and *young adolescents,* these principles could easily be adopted by a Community Learning Center serving students at any grade level.

Teacher as Researcher

When the school reform movement got started, one of the exciting concepts to emerge was the *teacher as researcher.* Teachers in a few schools were encouraged to work together to study the way they were teaching. They looked at their curriculum, their work environment, how they work with parents and the community, and the teaching methods they were using. The kind of research they were doing is often referred to as *action research*.

Action research often finds a home in schools that have *site-based, shared decision making*. As teachers become more empowered to participate in decision making, they want to be in a position to make more informed decisions. A group of teachers from New Mexico (Fischer et al., 2000, p. 2) described how they came together to launch teacher research in their schools.

> Teacher-research, as an intentional and systematic study of our own classrooms and schools, is an emergent approach to study *in situ*—and by the insiders—the educational phenomena taking place in the schools and classrooms. This approach is an *Inside Out* way of producing educational knowledge; that is, from inside the schools out toward the educational community. This is radically opposed to the traditional *Outside In* flow of knowledge that is from academia toward the schools and teachers. We [feel] that the ideal flow of educational knowledge should be both *Inside Out* and *Outside In*.

With knowledge coming from within the Community Learning Center, as well as from outside, a course can be charted toward improving the quality of education for all learners.

Teachers and Partnerships

The last area to be addressed in this chapter is teachers' role in the development of partnerships in the Community Learning Center. There are two distinct types of partnerships, those with the community and those with parents and families. Both will be discussed in detail later, but this might be a good place to talk about the role of teachers.

In many traditional schools the job of developing partnerships in the community is often left to administrators (both building level and central office). One result of that process is that when it comes time to sit down with the potential partners to discuss what they can do for the school, and what the school can do for them, there is an important element missing.

That critical element is the teachers who design and deliver the instruction. As a result, many of the partnerships that have been established in those schools have not always addressed issues critical to the mission of the school.

When teachers are involved in all phases of partnership development, there is a clear articulation between the academic needs of the students and the assistance a partnership can provide. This does not mean that administrators are incapable of knowing about the teaching and learning needs. It just means that involving teachers allows one more clear voice at the table to speak to the needs of students.

The Community Learning Center is organized to allow teachers the opportunity to be released from time to time to work on partnership development. This also encourages the teachers to maintain a strong network in the community. Teachers become aware of potential partnerships through their interactions with the parents and families of their students. Often a mother, father, or other family member will be employed in a business, agency, or community organization that has an interest and has resources to form an important partnership. If teachers are not encouraged to be a part of the partnership process, some potential partners may get away.

Clearly, the way the Community Learning Center approaches the teaching and learning process is a departure from what can be found in many traditional schools. The key to this approach is the development of a learning community in the center. Learning communities allow for the advancement of the collective knowledge and skills of the entire group. This creates a culture in the center that supports and nurtures knowledge building, creating a learning organization that will continue to learn and build capacity within the center.

Families as Partners

Several years ago I was asked to facilitate a meeting to bring together the many national organizations that were advocates for increasing the involvement of parents in their children's education. At the first meeting one of the participants suggested that we should drop the term *parent* from our discussions. The reason she gave made really good sense. She said, "We ought to be focusing on families because for many children in this country the significant adult in their lives may not be a parent. It may be a grandparent, an aunt or uncle, or even an older sibling." This shift in terminology helped us to recast the discussion about how to best develop a positive support system for children. I still find myself moving back and forth between the terms *parent* and *family*, but I almost always I remember in time to correct myself.

We are seeing tremendous emphasis being placed on student achievement as a measure of success in education. A significant research base shows us that there is a positive impact on student achievement where parents, families, and communities are involved in the education of our children. Anne Henderson and Karen Mapp (2002, p. 24) recently completed a synthesis of research in this area. From their review of 80 studies that were selected using rigorous research criteria, one overarching conclusion emerged:

> Taken as a whole, these studies found a positive and convincing relationship between family involvement and benefits for students, including improved academic achievement. This relationship holds across families of all economic, racial/ethnic and educational backgrounds and for students of all ages. Although there is less research on the effects of community involvement, it also suggests benefits for schools, families, and students, including improved achievement and behavior.

One researcher, Delores Peña (2000, p. 46), found that parent involvement was greatly influenced by the school staff taking the time to gain the trust of parents and inform them of how they can be involved. She provided suggestions for improving parent involvement.

- Make the parents feel more welcome.
- Change the attitudes of school staff so that they recognize the advantages of teachers and parents working together.

- ◆ Consider the educational level, language, culture, and home situation of parents.
- ◆ Give teachers time to plan and organize parent activities.
- ◆ Take parents' interests and needs into consideration when planning activities.
- ◆ Recognize that even if parents cannot be present at school, helping their children at home is also a valuable contribution.
- ◆ Provide parents with knowledge about how to be involved in a range of involvement opportunities.

Adding one additional element to this list would provide any school an excellent template for creating an effective program of parent and family involvement. That element is an ongoing program of providing two-way communication between the classroom and home. Kenneth LaLonde, one of my doctoral students, shared some tools developed by one of the elementary teachers is his school district. One in particular caught my attention as a means to communicate regularly with the home about the progress of the student. Judy Regenbogen, a teacher in the Manasas City Public Schools, Manasas, Virginia, developed the Student Progress Report shown here.

Figure 2.1. Student Progress Report

Progress Report

Week of: *April 7–11*

Name: _____

Academics:

We are working on fractions/decimals in Math. She continues to have difficulty with those multiplication facts. Please

Daily Skills: *continue to review facts 0 → 12 at home.*

Our focus has been quality work; with the development of organizational skills and homework return.

Positive Attitude:

Be proud of your work! Always try to give your best!   *Math Homework → 90%*
    Word study → 92%

News: *We will finish our Social Studies unit on ancient Greece and Rome. Look for study guide coming home! We continue to work on our Matter unit in Science.*

My thoughts about the week: _____

_____

_____

_____

> ### *The Challenge*
> It has often been said that we should not blame parents
> for the lack of progress of their children because they are
> sending us the best kids they have. We also need to keep
> in mind that parents and families care about their chil-
> dren and want them to be successful. The challenge to
> the Community Learning Center is to provide all the
> support that can be mustered to help parents and fami-
> lies as they raise their children. It will take a high level of
> commitment from everyone on the center's staff to make
> this happen, but the effort will pay off in terms of higher
> student achievement.

References

Bengier, A. L. (2000). *How one middle school began to plan for instruction: An action research journey.* Unpublished dissertation. Blacksburg, VA: Virginia Polytechnic Institute &
State University. (Available online at http://scholar.lib.vt.
edu/theses/available/etd-06292000–11080046/).

Center for Collaborative Education (2000, Fall). Turning
points core principles guide schools' work. *Conversations,
1*(1).

Darling-Hammond, L. (1993). Reframing the school reform
agenda. *Phi Delta Kappan,* June.

Dewey, J. (1897, January 16). My pedagogic creed. *The School
Journal, LIV*(3): 77–80.

Fischer, D., Mercado, M., Morgan, V., Robb, L., Sheehan-Carr,
J., & Torres, M. (2000, April). The curtain rises: Teachers un-
veil their processes of transformation in doing classroom
inquiry. *Networks: An On-line Journal for Teacher Research,
203*(1).

Gardner, H. (1999). *Frames of mind: The theory of multiple
intelligences.* New York: Basic Books.

Henderson, A., & Mapp, K. (2002). *A new wave of evidence: The
impact of school, family, and community connections of student*

achievement. Austin, TX: National Center for Family & Community Schools.

Peña, D. C. (2000). Parent involvement: Influencing factors and implications. *The Journal of Educational Research, 94*(1): 42–54.

Wheelock, A. (2000, Fall). Professional collaboration to improve teacher and student work. *Conversations, 1*(1).

3

Classrooms in the Community

Journey into Community

It is just past 10 o'clock in the morning. Into the main office of the Community Learning Center rushes young woman dressed in a smart business suit. She says that she is afraid that she is late because it was so hard to find a parking place. After pinning her community partner ID card to her lapel, she is off to the math department classrooms. She enters one of the classrooms, where she joins the teacher, already preparing for the instruction to be done in the coming period. It turns out that the woman is a math professor at a nearby university. She is there to team-teach a ninth grade algebra class. This is part of a yearlong program to see how some of the resources used to teach college math courses could help with high school students who have been struggling with algebra.

Down the hall a group of students in a biology class are involved in a very intense conversation with a man who isn't even in the room. He appears on the screen of a portable unit that allows the class to conduct an interactive videoconference with a water-quality specialist who works for the state Department of Environmental Quality. His office is in the state capital, halfway across the state from the classroom. The topic of their discussion is the impact that the water quality in a stream near the school has on the fish and wildlife in the surrounding area. This conversation has taken place once a week for the past three weeks. Students have been collecting data from the stream, and the scientist has been helping them in the analysis of that data. The study that the students are making of the stream will be helpful to the Department of Environmental Quality, which is currently short of staff to collect field data. The students are learning a lot about how water quality effects living things, and the state is getting help in collecting some important data. Of course, the content of what the students are learning has been correlated with the Standards of Learning tests that will come later in the year.

"The community is a classroom, and the classroom should be a community." My students have heard me say this so many times that they are probably sick of hearing it. But, it seems to make so much sense that we use the rich resources in the community to help our kids learn what they need to know to be successful when they take their places in that very same community.

A Student's View of Community-Based Learning

In my community experience, I went from learning what something is to applying it to real life. I learned why I need to know the things that I learned in math class. I had a chance to work with some neat people who let me try out things for myself. The mentor really seemed to care about me as a person, and I had fun.

Source: Comment by a student, cited in Owens & Wang, 1997, p.1.

The relationship of the school to the community comes into sharp focus when we read William Carr's (1942, p. 34) now-famous writing on schools as islands. He writes about schools being isolated from their communities, and about drawbridges being lowered in the morning so that the children of the mainland can come over to the island.

> Why do these young people go out to the island? They go there in order to learn how to live on the mainland. When they reach the island, they are provided with a supply of excellent books that tell about life on the mainland. They read these books diligently, even memorizing parts of them. Then they take examinations on them.

> Once in a while, as a special treat, the bus takes a few of the more fortunate or favored islanders on a hasty tour through the mainland itself. But it is very rare and is allowed to occur when the reading of the books about the mainland has been thoroughly completed.

How many schools today have a moat that children must cross each morning that keeps them apart from the mainland community? How many schools depend on children reading books about the mainland rather than experiencing the mainland itself? What must be done to drain the moat and get rid of the drawbridge? This chapter will provide some direction for taking the classroom into the community and bringing the community into the classroom.

Bringing the Community into the Classroom

Many schools have made a great deal of progress in finding ways to use community resources in their classrooms, so this is probably a safe place to start. You will find here examples of how Community Learning Centers go about expanding the use of community resources.

What is Needed?

Obviously, we don't need to replicate resources that are already present in the Community Learning Center. Teachers know how to design learning activities for students. They know the content they are responsible for teaching, and they know how to measure student growth. However, they may need help with getting students to see how what they are learning in classrooms is relevant to life in the community. There is that age-old question, "Why do I have to learn the difference between a noun and a pronoun?" Or, "Where will I ever need to conjugate verbs when I get out of school?"

The community can help bring subject matter alive by showing students how the knowledge and skills they are learning in the classroom can be applied to life in the community. This can be accomplished by involving willing partners from the community to create learning opportunities for students that will allow them to make real-world connections to what they are supposed to be learning in the classroom. It is not enough to tell kids that they need to know this because it is going to be on the statewide, standardized test that they are going to be taking five months down the road. If we can show that it is important to know how to do things to become successful in life, then students will become more focused on the learning process.

Educators must lead the way in opening the doors of the Community Learning Center to allow resources of the community to flow into classrooms to support student learning. Ernest Melby, an early pioneer in the field of Community Education once wrote; "It's the totally mobilized community we need. And in building one, educators will carve out a new role for themselves. We have been small and obscure—now we must be large and public" (Kerensky, 2002, p. 6).

Intergenerational Learning

Students in our classrooms also need to learn from the experiences of the older members of the community. Today we live in an information-rich society. In a typical week our kids have access through the Internet, television, and other media to more information that their grandparents had in a decade of their lives. Today's kids are information rich but experience poor. They may not have the opportunity to do as much, or exerience as much, as their grandparents did when they were children.

While many youth have been sitting in front of computers and televisions, their elders, when they were kids, were out doing things and gaining experiences firsthand. The Community Learning Center finds ways to bring together kids, who are rich in information but poor in experience, with older community members, who may be rich in experience but poor in information. It could be set up as a *learning exchange*. One successful example of a learning exchange is Kentucky's SOS (Share Our Skills) Program.

On a typical day, kids might be sitting in computer labs with grandparents showing them how to access a huge world of information through the Internet. Later in the afternoon those same kids might be down the street learning how to build a wooden boat or make an emergency shelter without a tent. This Cooperative Extension Service program in Kentucky was designed to make this exchange of knowledge and skills happen. Extension agents work with educators in schools to match curricular needs with available volunteers from the community. This allows the Extension to assist teachers who don't have the time or the contacts to reach out into the community to mobilize the talents that are available to help kids learn.

Programs like SOS could be established as a partnership venture between the Community Learning Center and agencies like Cooperative Extension. While we are focusing on Cooperative Extension, it would be good to emphasize what a useful ally it can be in the area of community learning. Extension agents are found in every state in the country, with offices in most every county and city. They are called Cooperative Extension because they were originally established as a partnership between the U.S. Department of Agriculture and the local governments, through the state land-grant universities.

Many educators, especially those in urban areas, have not sought out assistance from the Cooperative Extension because they expect it to only address agriculture or rural issues. The reality is that Extension has a wide array of resources and programs for audiences of all ages and interests (rural, urban, or suburban). What they don't have, in most cases, are facilities to use in delivering programs and services. They rely on a variety of community agencies and organizations to provide space for meetings of youth clubs (4-H), family, and adult programs. They can be a valuable partner in providing programs and services in the Community Learning Center.

What Resources Are Available?

Some educators are guilty of not seeing the forest for the trees when it comes to community resources that could be engaged in enhancing student learning. It takes a conscious effort to stand back and look at the community with an eye for what could be connected with learning in classrooms. We have been using a process of Community Resource Mapping to help discover resources that have not been yet been tapped. The process is rather simple, and it can be done in a couple of hours or less. Here are some step-by-step directions on how to go about using the process in your school community.

Community Resource Mapping

Step 1: Convene a wide range of stakeholders from the school community. This group could include teachers, students, parents, business people, community leaders, staff from community agencies, public-office holders, and community planners. You should invite from 30 to 40 people, but the group could be larger.

Step 2: Arrange the room with tables and chairs that can accommodate small group meetings. At the front of the room, place an enlarged map (about 48 by 60 inches, or larger) of the area served by the Community Learning Center. These maps could be hand-drawn using a smaller map as a model, or you may be able to get copies of large maps from local government planning offices. The map should be cut into four equal quadrants and temporarily joined on the front wall.

Step 3: Ask everyone in the audience to pretend that they are in a very slow airplane or helicopter flying in the sky over your community. Then say, "As you look down, think about the things you are seeing with the idea in mind that you are looking for resources that have potential to be involved in the learning that takes place in the Community Learning Center." Encourage them to use their imagination and not be limited to connections or partnerships that have existed in the past.

Step 4: Divide the participants into four groups. Each group will take one quadrant of the map, along with a set of colored marking pens. A facilitator should be chosen from the members of each of the four groups.

Step 5: Suggest that each person take some time (about 10 minutes) and make some notes on a 8.5 by 11 inch version of the community map quadrant assigned to their group. Individuals should start identifying all the resources they saw in their aerial trip over the community. Each resource should be physically located on the map.

Step 6: Within each group the facilitator should ask each member to share one of the resources he or she has located on the map. A recorder can locate and label those resources on the large map. Keep going around the group until every member's list is exhausted. Then ask the group to take a look at the map and try to see what might be missing.

Step 7: After a break, the groups reassemble, and the maps are joined once again on the front wall. Each group is then given time to report on the resources they located. The full group can then be asked what might be missing after each group has reported.

Step 8: The meeting is closed with an invitation for all those who are interested to attend a follow-up meeting, which will be held to design an action plan for approaching and engaging the potential partners that were identified during the Community Resource Mapping Process.

(This process was developed and tested by the National Association of Partners in Education and presented here with modifications by the author.)

The product of the mapping activity is a new level of awareness about the potential for connecting community resources with what is being done for kids in classrooms. People come up with potential partners that had not ever been considered in the past. It also serves as an excellent vehicle to bring people into the planning process for what goes on in the Community Learning Center.

Connecting Community-Based Learning to Academic Programs

The Southwest Educational Development Laboratory (SEDL) has done a lot of work in helping schools develop closer ties to the communities they serve. A recent newsletter from SEDL highlighted community-based learning. They considered traditional learning as being classroom- and text-book-bound, with a student's measure of success coming in the form of a test score. In contrast, they provided a look at an alternative.

> Community-based instruction, though it matches the characteristics of what we know about the most effective way of teaching, is messier and more complicated than this traditional model. Subject matter isn't easily segregated, the learning environment isn't rigidly controlled, and knowledge develops as much from student dialogue and problem solving as it does from the teacher or test.

They go on to talk about learning in which one student tutors another, or students collect samples from local streams and wells to monitor water quality, or students help to remodel the kitchen of an elderly resident. One question that immediately emerges is, will students learn academic subject matter as well? Or, more directly, will students perform well on the mandated achievement tests given by the state. With careful planning and reinforcement designed to make connections with academic subjects, students will learn. In most cases, teachers find that their students are more engaged in subject matter learning when they see an immediate use for their academic knowledge.

The other issue that is generally raised when community-based instruction is being considered is whether students can be trusted to make useful choices in helping to direct their own learning. The Southwest Educational Development Laboratory continues the list to include the following questions:

- ♦ Can they be helpful, attentive members of a collaborative group?
- ♦ Can they handle the responsibilities of working in the community?
- ♦ Can they manage complex projects where others depend on them?

The answer is a resounding "yes." Students can accept responsibility. In fact, many students are hungry for these kinds of activities, once they see a connection to their own lives and interests.

Community Lessons

Learn and Serve America is a federally supported initiative to advance service-learning as educational methodology. Service-learning is a concept that has been around for several years and has been implemented in many communities. The Corporation for National and Community Service was established by the federal government in 1993 to promote service learning opportunities for children and youth. The Corporation's website (http:www.learnandserve.org) provides a lot of good information about service-learning. The following is their definition of service-learning.

Service-Learning:

♦ Is a method whereby students learn and develop through active participation in thoughtfully organized service that is conducted in and meets the needs of communities

♦ Is coordinated with an elementary school, secondary school, institution of higher education, or community service program and the community

♦ Helps foster civic responsibility

♦ Is integrated into and enhances the academic curriculum of the students, or the education components of the community service program in which the participants are enrolled

♦ Provides structured time for students or participants to reflect on the service experience

One important key to the success of these programs has been the high level of integration with the curriculum in classrooms. In addition to developing academic skills, students develop practical skills, self-esteem, and a sense of civic responsibility.

A national study of Learn and Serve America programs suggests that effective service-learning programs:

♦ Improve grades

♦ Increase attendance

♦ Develop personal and social responsibility

The Massachusetts Department of Education has produced an outstanding curriculum guide containing 14 promising practices that illustrate how the community can be actively involved in student's learning. The guide was produced as part of the Massachusetts Learn and Serve America project. The introduction to the guide provides a context for the work that Massachusetts has done in this area.

> As a new millennium begins, we must ask how, as educators, we can sustain dynamic learning practices amid the pressures of accountability, increasingly diverse student populations, and a growing alienation and disengagement among many young people. Several schools in Massachusetts and across the nation have turned to Community Service Learning (CSL) to meet these multiple challenges. Increasingly, educators credit CSL with engaging students of various abilities and learning styles; fostering a healthy balance between a young person's individual aspirations and his or her responsibility as a productive citizen; and reducing age barriers that tend to isolate youth from older citizens in the community. (Bartsch, 2001, p. vii)

The promising practices are presented as 14 lessons developed and implemented by classroom teachers. Each of the lesson units presented describes:

♦ The rationale for connecting academic content to Community Service Learning activities

♦ Ways to assess academic and community outcomes

♦ Multiple connections to various Framework Learning Standards

♦ Community partners

♦ Lesson plans

♦ Solutions to organizational barriers

♦ Time lines

♦ Resources and materials

♦ Goals for the future

One of the most powerful outcomes reported in the Massachusetts CSL experience was a shift in the community's perception of schools and students.

> Many community members only see schools as a tax burden and students as "rascals" to be controlled until adulthood. Communities don't generally think of students and classrooms as potential resources for addressing the issues of the community. CSL changes these perceptions by encouraging students to move from being passive observers of the community to active contributors. (Bartsch, 2001, p. ix)

Sample Community Service-learning Lessons

Safety on the Bus

The third graders in Brayton Elementary School decided that they had had enough of being tormented by bullies on the school bus. They enlisted the help of fifth graders to interview students, school administrators, and personnel from the bus company to better understand the problems of safety on the school bus. In the process of collecting data, they discovered strategies for improving their own behavior and ways to make the buses throughout the city more user friendly.

"I learned you need to stay out of other people's business. I've also learned to respect other people's feelings. I dislike when other people use foul language. I think the bullies should lay off the younger kids. They shouldn't take their anger out on the kids when it happens at home."

Fifth grade student
Brayton Elementary

Ordinary Heroes

The Ordinary Heroes Project was a cross-age project that combined a fifth grade class with a ninth grade English class to find ordinary citizens who have made extraordinary contributions to their community. Ordinary Heroes was a full-year project. The classes met every two weeks to establish criteria and an interview process for the various citizens who qualified as potential Ordinary Heroes. The combined classes were divided into seven groups, half fifth graders and half ninth graders, for mentoring to develop between older and younger students. As a result of the yearlong project, the students gained a greater understanding of the complexities of managing a small town like the one they lived in and an awareness of the amount of volunteer work performed by citizens to keep town programs running smoothly.

> "At the beginning of the year, I believed that someone who encountered a dilemma and acted on instinct was a true hero. . . . I eventually realized that the best heroes are known only by their closest friends and family as they do deeds quietly and modestly, hoping to go unnoticed.... A hero needs to be selfless in all acts that he/she encounters to qualify as a true hero."
>
> *Ninth grade student*
> *Sharon High School*

The project culminated with a ceremony where the 10 Ordinary Heroes selected by the students were presented with certificates at a reception honoring them and their families. The names of the heroes are on the Ordinary Heroes Hall of Fame plaque, which hangs in the town's public library.

Senior–Senior Prom

The senior sociology classes have traditionally examined, through textbook readings, an issue related to elderly in society. The seniors at Drury High School, seeking a greater understanding of the problems facing this population, choose to relate to senior citizens firsthand. Students visited adult daycare centers, senior citizen centers, and nursing homes. During weekly visits they played cards, exchanged stories, and witnessed firsthand the concerns of senior citizens in today's society. In celebration of "bridging the gap" between the generations, the senior class and the senior citizens coplanned a Senior–Senior Prom.

"Through my experiences in the recreational therapy department at the nursing home, I have learned many lessons that a classroom could not teach me. I learned compassion, sensitivity, and putting other people before yourself. As I grow up and leave Drury High School these lessons will help me in the world. Education cannot be limited to a few subjects. Responsibility and leadership have also been taught to me through Community Service Learning. Getting out into the community is exhilarating."

12th grade student
Drury High School

These outstanding learning activities are described in greater detail, along with a dozen more, in *Community Lessons.* This excellent book is available at no charge in a Portable Document Format (PDF) at the Massachusetts Department of Education's Community Service Learning website (http:www.doe.mass.edu/csl).

But, I Have to Get
These Kids Ready for the Tests!

So far we have looked at using community resources in helping students learn and understand why it is important to learn what they are being taught. We have looked at the potential of Community Service Learning in extending students' experiences beyond knowledge of content to being able to make practical applications of knowledge and develop civic responsibility. But, and this is a big but, teachers are feeling pressure to narrow what is being taught to what is being tested. This may result in a test-driven curriculum that is considerably more narrow than many of us would like to see in our classrooms.

There is no clear consensus in our country about the role of standardized testing in the movement to improve the quality of education for our children. In the 33rd Annual Phi Delta Kappan/Gallup Poll of the Public's Attitudes Toward the Public Schools (Rose & Gallup, 2001) there are data showing how diverse are the attitudes on standardized testing.

When asked about the emphasis being placed on testing, 31 percent responded that there is too much emphasis; 22 percent, not enough emphasis; 44 percent, just about the right amount of emphasis; and 3 percent didn't know. Over a three-year span these percentages have shifted a little, with those who felt there was too much emphasis gaining 11 percentage points, and the not-enough emphasis group losing 6 percentage points.

Further confusing messages are sent by the 12th conclusion reached in the PDK/Gallup Study where Americans offered narrow support for the use of a single test in making decisions regarding grade-to-grade promotion and graduation, but they rejected such tests in favor of classroom work and homework when it comes to measuring student achievement (65 percent classroom work/homework to 35 percent test scores).

Aligning Community Resources with Curriculum

When standardized testing first swept the landscape of schools in this country, we saw a rapid movement to align the curriculum with what was being tested. In some states this was not easy, since the tests were often based on a new set of expectations of students that were not addressed by the curriculum. This had a big impact on teachers and textbook publishers. Teachers were scrambling to find teaching resources that matched the tests that their students would have to take and pass. Textbook publishers were faced with many states developing their own tests, which often emphasized different content.

All of this meant that teachers became busy trying to make sure that the textbooks and other teaching materials were properly aligned with standardized tests. This resulted in less time being available to connect community resources to teaching in the classroom.

One key to success in the Community Learning Centers is in staffing. Each center has a staff person who is responsible for working with teachers to identify areas in the curriculum where community resources might enhance the instruction. That person, the Community Education Coordinator, is also the one who moves about the community to locate resources that can be used to help students to become successful in achieving at high levels on standardized test. All of this requires a great deal of communication between the teaching faculty and the Community Education Coordinator to make sure that learning objectives are the focus of all learning activities involving community resources.

The major image to keep in focus is that of schools as islands, set aside from their communities by moats of convention and tradition. Community Learning Centers are firmly placed at the center of the community, with no moats or drawbridges separating them from their communities. The payoff is that the education of our children becomes a major community priority that brings together the resources needed to provide the kind of education our children will need to become successful in the 21st century.

Schoolhouse Education Inadequate

"Community education has recognized that education must be lifelong, that it is for young and old. Equally important, community educators have become aware of the tremendous educational resources of the community. Thus experience with community education has simultaneously deepened understanding of the educational process, revealed the inadequacy of a schoolhouse concept of education, shown the need for lifelong education, and revealed the richness of the resources available for building a truly great education."

(Kerensky, 2002, p. 10)

References

Bartsch, J. (2001). *Community lessons: Promising curriculum practices.* Boston: Massachusetts Department of Education (available in PDF format at http:www.doe.mass.edu/csl/comlesson.pdf).

Carr, W. (1942). *Community life in a democracy.* Chicago: National Association of Parents and Teachers.

Kerensky, V. M. (Ed.) (2002). *The Ernest O. Melby Papers.* Boca Raton, FL: Florida Atlantic University.

Owens, T.R., & Wang, C. (1997). *Community-based learning: A foundation for meaningful educational reform.* Portland, OR: Northwest Regional Education Laboratory (School Improvemnt Research Series).

Rose, C. R., & Gallup, A. M. (2001, September). The 33rd annual Phi Delta Kappa/Gallup Poll of the public's attitudes toward the public schools. *Phi Delta Kappan, 83*(1): 41–58.

4

Teacher Leadership

Journey into Community

It is Thursday night, and the Community Learning Center Council is about to be called into session. The facilitator this month is math teacher Bonnie Fuller. Bonnie has been a member of the council since the transition was made from a traditional school to a Community Learning Center. In the early years she was instrumental in helping to obtain a grant to get things started. Now she is part of the team that helps to make decisions about how the center operates. Her job tonight as facilitator is one that rotates among all the members.

One role that Bonnie plays on the council is to represent the teaching faculty in the center. She also represents teachers who are involved in the family literacy program and other adult education programs offered in the center.

On another visit to the center we may want to sit in on a teaching team meeting that is led by teachers, even though the assistant principal sits in as a member of the team. This team is currently involved in an action research project to look at various ways that they might improve instruction for fourth graders who did not do well in the last state testing period.

Throughout the center there are faculty involved in various committees and task forces. One group involving teachers, parents, and community leaders is planning a big celebration to mark the opening day of school next fall. The idea was introduced by a teacher taught in a school where the opening day celebration had been very effective in getting kids excited about school and generating a great show of support from parents and the community.

Teachers are also actively involved in mentoring new teachers and supporting the continuous improvement of those teachers who are veterans but still learning. The focus in the center is on being a community of learners, where everyone is continually involved in learning.

Roland Barth (2001, p. 445), founder of the Harvard Principals' Center, did an excellent job in summing up what is at stake in teachers becoming leaders when he wrote,

> All teachers have leadership potential and can benefit from exercising that potential. Teachers become more active learners in an environment where they are leaders. When teachers lead, principals extend their own capacity, students enjoy a democratic community of learners, and schools benefit from better decisions. This is why the promise of widespread teacher leadership in our schools is so compelling for principals, students and teachers and for the success of schools themselves.

In 1976, I was working as a visiting professor at a state college in Ballarat, Australia. While I was in the country I became aware of a movement called *Democratization of the Workplace* that was underway in the state of South Australia. It was the brainchild of Premier Anthony Dunston. The media often portrayed him as a bright, but slightly eccentric, leader. Since this period of time was at the height of the cold war, there were some critics who labeled the movement a prelude to communism. People were nervous when the talk drifted to things like *worker empowerment* and *shared power*. I had some reservations myself until I learned what they were trying to accomplish.

Democratization of the Workplace represented the very opposite of how we had all come to understand the way organizations worked. We had been accustomed to a "command-and-control" style of organization, where all the power to make decisions about how the organization accomplished its work resided in the designated leaders. That translated to mean the *bosses.*

In schools, at that period of time, principals were the ones who made decisions in schools. Those decisions included hiring teachers, teacher assignment, budgeting resources, and student discipline.

After I returned home from my short stay in Australia, I began to see some of the elements of workplace democratization showing up in U.S. schools. We would come to recognize this movement with the label, "site-based management." As part of this movement we began to see teachers emerging as leaders. With many of the decisions about things that happen at the school site being moved out of the central office and into the school, there was the potential for teacher empowerment. The word *potential* should be emphasized. The realization of teacher empowerment was dependent on two essential elements.

First, the orientation and training of the principal was (and still is) a critical issue in the sharing of decision-making power with teachers. Principals who were highly successful under the old command-and-control environment were reluctant to give up what they perceived as a style that had worked well for them in the past. Many of these principals were prepared with skills that were designed to manage and administer a school. As a point of reference, most university programs preparing principals were located in Departments of Educational Administration. Now, most of these departments have become Departments of Educational Leaders. This was a change in semantics, of course, but also a very significant indicator of a shift in the role of principals and in the way they are being prepared to do the job.

The second issue impacting teacher empowerment was the leadership at the top of the organization, represented by the superintendent. Superintendents were being pressured by many sources to move more decision making to the school site. Some of this pressure came from school board members who work in industries where worker empowerment has been successfully in place for several years. The experience of business and industry had led these school board members to see empowering teachers to participate in the decision-making process as a way to bring about change in the schools. The problem we have today was created by the accountability system that had been in place for years. In that system principals are typically called to the superintendent's office for an annual review of the progress of students in their school. This created an atmosphere among principals that was summed up by one of the principals in our doctoral program a few years ago. He said, "I am not opposed to site-based management, but if my butt is on the line, then I am going to make those final decisions myself." He went on to say that he would certainly support more of a voice for teachers and parents, but after listening to those voices he would make the final decision. My suggestion to him was to ask to take along the members of his school improvement council the next time he was called on to account for the performance of his students. The rationale for bringing them along is simple. If they are going to share the decision making, then they need to share the accountability.

The Culture of the School

The movement toward empowering teachers is deeply embedded in the culture of the Community Learning Center. The centers have a strong foundation in a culture that encourages teacher leadership. This does not mean that the head of the learning center doesn't have a responsibility to lead, but it does mean that the nature of that leadership may be vastly different than what we saw in schools of the past.

A report of the American Youth Policy Forum, *High Schools of the Millennium* (2000, p. 17), addressed the problem of the barriers created by school leaders using approaches from the past.

> Too often, administrators maintain the hierarchical structure of schools, keeping decision making under their control, to avoid any controversy or challenge to authority. This environment creates difficulty for teachers, parents, and other community leaders interested in innovation and risk taking.

This old culture also has teachers teaching behind closed doors, having little communication about their work with colleagues. Communication with parents is too often limited to open-house programs and a few brief parent-teacher conferences.

Time as a Precious Resource

Time is a very precious quantity in schools. As Barth (2001, p. 445) writes, "it is in finite supply and in infinite demand." Many of my graduate students in recent years have done research on how change takes place in schools. One of the universal findings to come out of most of those studies has been the importance of time as a resource for teachers to reflect, plan, interact, and be part of the leadership of the school. A look at a typical school day quickly reveals the nature of the problem.

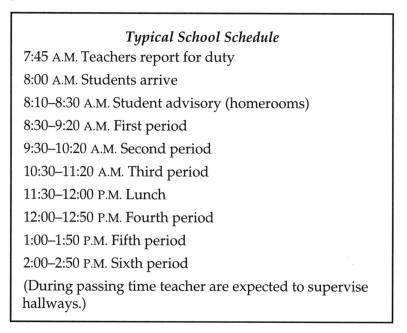

Typical School Schedule

7:45 A.M. Teachers report for duty

8:00 A.M. Students arrive

8:10–8:30 A.M. Student advisory (homerooms)

8:30–9:20 A.M. First period

9:30–10:20 A.M. Second period

10:30–11:20 A.M. Third period

11:30–12:00 P.M. Lunch

12:00–12:50 P.M. Fourth period

1:00–1:50 P.M. Fifth period

2:00–2:50 P.M. Sixth period

(During passing time teacher are expected to supervise hallways.)

In the example, a secondary school with a six-period day, teachers often would have the responsibility to be with students all day with the exception of one planning period. This problem is compounded even further in schools with a seven-period daily schedule. Most planning and communication involving teachers must be done before or after school. With the many tasks teachers have to address each day—grading papers, meeting with students and parents, keeping records, preparing instructional materials for class—there is little time left in the day for planning and leadership activities.

A look at a sample daily schedule for a Community Learning Center will show how time can be provided for teachers to be involved in communicating with colleagues and leadership activities in the school.

Community Learning Center Schedule

7:45 A.M. Teachers arrive

8:00 A.M. Students arrive

8:00–8:30 A.M. Student advisory team

8:30–9:50 A.M. First instructional block

10:00–11:20 A.M. Second instructional block

11:30–12:15 P.M. Lunch

12:20–1:30 P.M. Third Instructional Block

1:40–3:05 P.M. Fourth Instructional Block

3:15–5:00 P.M. Student enrichment/activity block

The block schedule and the use of a fifth period block for enrichment activities (not necessarily supervised by the regular day teachers) allow time for teachers to meet and plan with their colleagues. Each teacher would have classroom assignments during three of the four instructional blocks. Teams of faculty could use their fourth block as time to work on instructional planning, action research, or other staff-development activities. A principal in one of my classes commented that there would be a temptation to assign other duties to teachers during the time designed for planning. This practice could defeat the purpose of providing teachers with time to work together collaboratively.

The American Youth Policy Forum (2000, p. 36) also presents a recommendation to provide teachers with the time needed to build strong support networks in the school.

> [Schools should] provide space and time for teachers to meet often and to review and improve their

teaching strategies and increase student learning. Provide teachers support networks, pair new teachers with experienced teachers and provide follow-up coaching and technical assistance following in-service.

The Community Learning Center, because of its extended-year calendar, can set aside one day per month for centerwide and teacher-team planning. While this is happening, the students are involved in an extensive program of enrichment activities provided in collaboration with the center's partner agencies and organizations.

"We are losing many good teachers to other professions for a variety of reasons. Pay is the one that is most often heard, but I often think that lack of support and lack of time do their damage. If we collaborate with parents and community, some of these stresses would ease."

Source: Kathleen Skelding-Dills, classroom teacher enrolled in a School Community Partnerships Seminar at Virginia Tech, Summer 2001.

Deciding Which Reform Model

I have a classic case study that I often use in my classes to help prospective principals understand the importance of teachers having a voice in the major instructional decisions in the school. An elementary principal in a school in our area was feeling pressure from the school board and superintendent. The performance of the students on the standardized tests used by the state to measure student achievement at that school was lagging behind most of the schools in the district. This principal was directed to have the school adopt a reform model that would result in improvement in student performance.

The principal selected the *Success for All* approach to schoolwide reform. The designers of Success for All required an 80 percent favorable vote on the part of teachers before the program could be implemented. The principal was sure that the teachers would support the new initiative after some of them had a chance to see it in action. She sent teams of teachers to visit other schools around the state that had implemented the program.

The teams came back with some mixed reports. Some teachers liked what they saw; others were very negative about their experiences. The negative reports centered on the feature of the model that called for teachers to teach from a closely scripted instructional plan. As the teachers began to share their observations with other teachers in the school, it became clear that the required 80 percent vote was not going to happen. In fact, the vote came out 55 percent against Success for All, 45 percent for it—far short of the required 80 percent support needed.

The principal was portrayed by the local newspaper as being overwhelmed and disappointed with the teachers' decision. She was quoted as saying, "I thought I knew what I was doing, and all of a sudden I know nothing and I am starting from scratch and trying to figure all this out."

This case becomes a springboard for a rich discussion about how to go about implementing schoolwide change. One of the issues that always comes out in my students' analyses is that the teachers should have been given a greater voice early on in the process. They should have been involved in analyzing the problems they wanted to address by changing the way they taught the children in the school. My students also felt that the teachers should be involved in researching the wide array of *reform* models that have been put in place in schools around the country. Finally, teachers should be involved in selecting which model they want to implement and not called upon to validate a decision that had already been made by a principal.

Teachers Helping to Select New Teachers

I am continually amazed at the slow progress we have made in the process of involving teachers in helping to select their colleagues. That is one of the last vestiges of power for some principals. I often ask principals if they involve teachers in the selection process of new teachers. They often say, "Of course not, that is a management decision. Our school district wants the selection to be handled by principals and central office personnel." It seems to me that teachers are in an excellent position to know what to look for in new teaching colleagues, perhaps more than anyone in the schools.

There is also the issue of building a collaborative environment in the Community Learning Center. Teachers who have a role in helping to choose their colleagues also have an investment in helping to see that they are successful. With all that has been written about the importance of teachers, especially new teachers, having a mentor and support system to improve their teaching, it seems even more important to have a role for teachers in selecting new teachers for the school.

Career Paths for Teachers

Each year hundreds of teachers enroll in certification programs to become principals. Many of these teachers truly want to become principals; others look at the principalship as the next step to take to advance their career. This is especially true of young male teachers who feel that if they are to be successful, they must seek promotion to a principalship. This comes mostly from the fact that few schools offer a career path for career teachers.

A superintendent of one of the nation's largest school districts was recently heard to say that he was a big fan of the National Board Certification for teachers. He said, "This helps us to identify teachers who we can select to become principals in our schools."

Some teachers love what they do, and they are very good at it. They should not have to leave the field of teaching to experience some sense of career advancement or to provide leadership in their schools. The Community Leaning Center would offer a career ladder for teachers who aspire to advance. The career ladder would be the creation of the members of the school community, with the blessing of the school board and administration, of course.

Most career ladders include a role for the master teacher. Some of the typical roles for the master teacher include:

♦ Mentoring new teachers

- Providing coaching for teachers in need of improvement
- Demonstrating leadership in planning and helping to conduct staff development programs
- Sharing in teacher evaluation responsibilities
- Helping teachers to analyze and use data that give feedback on their teaching
- Developing and selecting new curriculum materials
- Helping in establishing effective community partnerships

This extensive list shows what kind of responsibility can be placed with master teachers. Each of the roles listed has the potential to have an important positive impact on student achievement.

How these master teachers would be selected, and how exactly they would fit into the pattern of staffing in the school is an issue that each Community Learning Center ought to be able to decide upon independently. Obviously, master teachers would be chosen from those who had demonstrated the greatest skill level in their own teaching. They would also need to have a class load that would allow them some release time to work with other teachers and in staff-development activities.

Should All Teachers Be Leaders?

Linda Lambert (1998, p. 42), in her book, *Building Leadership Capacity in Schools,* provided a good answer to the question, "Is it a goal that every educator become a leader?"

> Leaders are perceived as consummate learners who attend to the learning of both adults and children—including themselves, of course. This is what it should mean to be a professional educator. It does not mean that all leadership work will look the same. While some educators will chair committees and facilitate large-group meetings, others will focus their energies on implementing peer coach-

ing, team teaching, conducting collaborative action research, and demonstrating reflective practice.

The goal of the Community Learning Center is for every teacher to be given the opportunity, encouragement, and support to be a leader. The end result is as Barth (2001, p. 449) so eloquently put it, "Teachers become owners and investors in the school, rather than mere tenants. They become professionals."

Developing Teacher Leaders

- Identify and develop leaders in the Community Learning Center who might be interested and are capable of playing leadership roles. Teacher leaders often come from those most receptive to change, but other leaders may emerge as planning for change gains momentum.

- Use a team structure that is inclusive rather than exclusive. Establishing a team of individuals who are representative of the entire learning community will send the message that the process of planning for change is to be an inclusive process.

- Balance skills and styles within the leadership team. The most effective teams are those that take advantage of the expertise and skills that their members already have. Being able to match the right person with the right job makes a big difference to the success of the team.

- Make the roles, responsibilities, and expectations clear to everyone. Teacher leaders are often reluctant to step out of the comfort of their classrooms into the unknown of leadership in issues that extend throughout the learning community. They need to have an understanding of what is expected of them, what authority they have, what they can expect from the other members of the learning community, and what they can expect from other members of the leadership team.

> It is important that everyone in the Community
> Learning Center understands who the leadership
> team is, what their responsibilities are, and what they
> are trying to accomplish.
>
> ■ Facilitate the development of leadership skills. Even
> the most outstanding teachers will need support
> when moving into leadership positions in the Com-
> munity Learning Center. Resources need to be di-
> rected in providing support to these new leaders in
> learning effective group process practices, how to de-
> velop short- and long-term plans, and how to seek in-
> put from the range of stakeholders represented in the
> Community Learning Center.

What Happened to the Principal?

With all this attention on teacher leadership, we can't ne-
glect the issue of the overall leadership of the Community
Learning Center. Some centers have dropped the title of principal for the person who provides the overall leadership. To
maintain the title of principal carries an implication that the
leadership role is the same as in a traditional school. This is
not the case in the Community Learning Center. The leader
will have to be more of a facilitator who works at bringing
people together in teams to accomplish things they could not
accomplish working alone. The leader will have to be more of
a skilled collaborator who can establish partnerships and
links with key agencies, organizations, and families in the
community. The leader will still need to be an instructional
leader, but in that leadership role, it will be more important to
empower teachers to work together to improve instruction.
The other important leadership function in the center will be
for the leader to help build a shared vision that will drive
everything that is done in the center.

The hitch comes when trying to come up with a title for the
center's leader. My preference for titles at this point in time is
not in place in any Community Learning Center, to my knowl-

edge. That title is *Chief Learner Officer (CLO)*. What I think this implies is that there is someone who can help to create a true learning community, a community that is dedicated to the continuous learning of all members. This leadership title reinforces the idea of everyone being a learner in the Community Learning Center. Sure, this person will still have many of the administrative responsibilities that come with the operation of an education unit. Budgets, buses, food service, and equipment that needs repair will all remain on the agenda. But, the CLO title will not let the leader stray too far from the central mission of the Community Learning Center.

I know that many new Community Learning Centers have struggled with what to call the leader. Some have been forced by school district policy to continue to use the title principal. Perhaps, in those cases, they could make a small modification that would recognize a change in the role but meet the district policy. They could call their leader the *Principal Learner*. I suspect that as the Community Learning Center movement grows, we will see a wide variety of titles used. This is one of the beauties of the concept. There is room for each center to be different from one another in many ways.

References

American Youth Policy Forum (2000, August). *High schools of the millennium: Report of the workgroup.* Washington, DC: Author.

Barth, R. (2001, February). Teacher Leader. *Phi Delta Kappan 84*(10):443–449.

Lambert, L. (1998). *Building leadership capacity.* Alexandria, VA: Association for Curriculum Supervision and Development.

5

Partnerships for Student Success

Journey into Community

The Community Learning Center has just received the results of the state-mandated tests. Most of the results are excellent, but one set of scores stands out. The fourth grade reading test scores have fallen below the state minimum for the first time. The center's Steering Council decides it is time to get some help from the community to address this drop in reading scores.

The potential partners included the editor of the local newspaper, the community relations director for a large insurance company with headquarters in the community, and a representative of the PTA.

The fourth grade lead teacher began the meeting by saying that the teachers at his grade level felt that there was a need for some help for individual students who were struggling with reading. The insurance company representative suggested that her company would be interested in developing a tutoring program, and some of their employees would be willing to serve as tutors.

Next, the principal asked if there was a way to get families more engaged in their children's education. The PTA member jumped in to say that his Instructional Support Committee was already talking about starting a program called Families Reading for Excellence, which had been piloted by the National PTA.

Not wanting to be left out, the newspaper editor chimed in with an offer to start a Newspapers in the Classroom program that had been successful in many other communities. He was ready to offer free copies of papers for classroom use and training for teachers in how to tie them into their instructional program.

From all this, the Reading Excellence Partnership was formed. This partnership brings together a variety of powerful resources focused on working with teachers and students to raise student reading test scores.

Charles S. Mott, Michigan industrialist and major benefactor of the Community Education movement, was often quoted as saying, "We must all live in partnership with our communities." He certainly did that through the work he did to make his community and many communities across the country better places to live. The ultimate success of the Community Learning Center is highly dependent on how effective its leaders are in establishing partnerships with the community.

In 2000 the National Association of Partners in Education reported that 69 percent of the school districts nationwide engaged in partnerships activities, compared with 51 percent in 1990. These statistics came from a study conducted to monitor the growth of partnerships. The study, *Partnerships 2000: A Decade of Growth and Change,* documented a lot of progress, but we know that schools still have human, financial, and material needs far greater than the resources federal, state, and local governments can allocate to meet those needs (National Association of Partners in Education, 2002b).

Educators today are facing enormous challenges in helping all students succeed in the current environment of high-stakes testing and accountability, growing student diversity, and increased stress on family structures. Partnerships offer a source for obtaining the kind of support from the community that often can make the difference between many children and young people being successful or left behind.

Who are the Partners?

It is important at this point to identify who is it we are talking about when we talk about school community partners. When they hear the term *educational partnership,* some people immediately think of partnerships between schools and businesses in the community. That is certainly not untrue, as businesses make up an important segment of the partnerships that are helping to support student success. But, there is another equally important set of partners we need to acknowledge. Those partners are the families of the students we serve in our schools.

Joyce Epstein (2001, p. 4) makes a good case for comprehensive partnerships to support children.

> In partnership, educators, families, and community members work together to share information, guide students, solve problems, and celebrate success. Partnerships recognize the shared responsibility of home, school, and community for children's learning and development. Students are central to successful partnerships.

She goes on to point out that every community has individuals and groups that care about children, share responsibilities for their futures, and have the potential to be valuable resources as partners with schools. This chapter will address issues that surround both partnerships with families and partnerships with the community, as the two often have very distinctive characteristics and require somewhat different strategies.

Focusing Partnerships on Student Success

As the standards-based movement picked up steam, principals and teachers around the country began to question the value of spending time on developing partnerships. They were saying things like, "Our kids didn't do well on last spring's state assessment tests. We can't be distracted by working on partnership; we have to be doing all we can to improve these test scores." Or, " Partnerships are nice, but we just don't see them having any impact on student achievement in our school." Also, "Why should we bother trying, parents don't really care." This represents what I call the "circle the wagons" mentality. It says that educators believe that all the resources they need to help students be successful reside right there, inside the school building, inside the four walls of the classroom and the two covers of the textbook. The reality is that most schools are desperately in need of help from any direction, and there are not enough resources to see to it that *All Children Are Learning* or *No Child Is Left Behind*.

To counter this potential retreat from partnering with the community, I developed an activity that was designed to focus partnerships on student achievement. In Virginia we have been working for several years under a system that requires our schools to prepare students to be successful on statewide, standardized tests that are given each spring. These standards are called Standards of Learning, or SOL. Many critics feel that these standards have narrowed the curriculum by having teachers focus only on those things that are to be tested. Many of the standards currently emphasize the memorization of facts, rather than problem solving or higher-order thinking.

The partnership planning activity involves bringing together teachers, parent, students, and leaders from the community. The group is first given some background on how important partnerships can be to the success of students in the Community Learning Center. The second step is to distribute copies of the current standards of learning that are being used in the state and some sample test questions. Once all the participants in the planning session have had a chance to look over the standards, they are given some specific standards to study. These standards are selected based on past performance results from the students in the center. Low performance indicates an area of instruction where students may need help.

The participants are divided into small groups that mix the different groups represented at the session. Each group is assigned specific learning objectives with the charge to use the worksheet to identify partners in the community who might be able to contribute to student success on that standard. See the worksheet that follows. As the groups begin to share what they know about the community and potential partners, the worksheet will guide the conversation. After about an hour, the groups each record the product of their work on a transparency version of the worksheet. The transparencies are then used in a presentation to the whole group.

Partnerships for Student Success

Learning Objective Selected:

List Potential Partner(s):

Goal of Partnership:

Possible Partnerships Activities:

Measures of Partnerships Success:

WIIFMs:

©Steve Parson, Falls Church, VA, 2000

There are several outcomes produced by this activity.

- Community participants and parents are often surprised when they get their first up-close look at what the students are being expected to learn.
- Many of the partnerships identified by the groups involve multiple partners working together.
- Potential partners that had never been considered before are uncovered.
- Roles for families as part of the partnerships begin to emerge.
- Educators begin to see connections between the instruction in the classroom and resources in the community that they have not seen before.
- The partnerships that are the product of the discussions of the small groups often go on to become a reality.

The process is used to create an awareness of the potential for participants that can be connected to student academic success and lead to the formation of new partnerships.

One thing that has become clear in the development of partnerships is that each party to the partnership must be able to identify something that they or their organization is getting out of being part of the partnership. For some businesses like banks, they gain visibility as an institution that makes a contribution to things the community cares about, like educating kids. It may be a direct benefit such as improving the quality of education to improve the quality of the new employees a company hires. For parents the benefits are more easily identified. All parents want the very best education for their children. And we cannot leave the schools out of the WIIFM game. Educators need to invest time to determine exactly what benefits they want to gain through the partnership. Without this attention to the WIIFMs, we often fail to design partnerships in a way that each party can get what they want out of the partnership.

WIIFMs

The acronym stands for What's In It For Me, which is a
shorthand way of referring to the fact that everyone is
motivated by what they can get out of any arrangement,
including a new partnership. It is important to identify
these factors at the very beginning of the process of developing a partnership.

A Partnership Development Model

For the past 15 years National Association of Partners in
Education,[1] a partnership advocacy organization, has been
developing and testing a model to guide the development of
effective educational partnerships. The model has seven steps
that provide a guide to the partnership development process.

---

1   The National Association of Partners in Education closed
    operations in January 2003.

Steps to Successful Partnership Development

- Creating a climate for success.

  Create awareness with key stakeholders within schools and the community about partnerships as a way to improving the schools and community.

- Assess needs and potential resources.

  Examine the needs that exist in the school community that are not currently being met with available resources. For example, create a map locating the resources that exist in the community that might be connected through partnerships to the work of the Community Learning Center.

- Exploring Partnerships Models

  Develop an inventory of current partnerships in place in the community. Seek information about other community partnership models that might serve as a guide.

- Developing Vision, Goals, Objectives, and Action Plans

  The vision becomes a shared view of the dream that describes where you would like to be at some point in the future. The goals, objectives, and action plans give the partners a road map for how to travel together to make the dream a reality.

- Developing the Management System

  At this point a written commitment between the policy makers of the partner organizations is created. A formal group should be developed with representatives from each of the stakeholder groups that will provide advice on the partnership's policy and management structure and help build support for the partnership's goals and objectives. A final management function is to market the partnership and it results. Successful partnerships are a good magnet for attracting additional new partners.

- Implementing the Programs

  A partnership involves resources from outside the school that must be managed properly to implement the programs developed in the action plan. These resources include not only financial, but also material and in-kind resources. They also include human resources in the form of volunteers with knowledge and experience that can have a positive impact on the lives of students.

- Monitoring and Evaluation

  All the partners will want to know how successful they are in accomplishing the goals that had been set. Monitoring is a way of gathering information on an ongoing basis to make midcourse corrections where they are needed, and to check for progress toward accomplishing the goals and objectives at an agreed-upon time. Establishing an evaluation plan has to be a priority for all the stakeholders who are involved in the partnership.

Source: National Association of Partners in Education (2002a)

Years of observing partnerships in schools across the country have led me to the conclusion that most partnerships are allowed to develop very informally, driven primarily by a desire to make a contribution to the work of the schools in educating children. As a result of this informal process, many partnerships lack a clear set of goals and no plan for how the outcomes of the partnership are to be measured. This brings to mind a scene from an old Abbot and Costello movie. The two are roaring down the road in an old open-roof automobile in a driving rainstorm, when the steering wheel comes off. Abbot asks Costello if he knows where they are. He replies, "No, but we're making darn good time." In a similar vein, *if you don't know where you are going, any road will do.*

Partnerships in the Community Learning Center need to be well focused to have a positive impact on student success.

They need to have in place a clear set of goals and objectives, with an action plan to guide the development of programs and activities sponsored by the partnership. Equally important to the sustainability of those partnerships is a good plan for evaluating the success of the partnership. Following the seven-step model will ensure that partnerships have a firm foundation to grow and serve the needs of students.

Partnership Portfolios

Portfolios have been used for several years to document and assess the work of students. In my own graduate classes I have been asking students to prepare a portfolio for each class they take with me. These portfolios will typically contain archives that include work products from class learning activities, reflections on their learning, readings, and examples of how they might have applied what they studied. In elementary and secondary schools student portfolios are used to examine growth and improvement over the course of a school year. From this background we have been working on a project to develop portfolios for school partnerships.

The idea is the same as with student portfolios, but with the focus on each of the partnerships serving a school. These portfolios serve several purposes. First, they function as an historical record of the partnership. It is troubling to find that may partnerships are so poorly documented that when one of the key leaders moves or changes jobs, the institution memory often goes with him or her.

The second purpose served by the portfolio is to create an awareness of the partnership within the school and the community. The last, and perhaps most important, function of the portfolio is to document the activities and accomplishments of the partnership. Most partnerships provide little feedback to their partners about the accomplishments that were outcomes of their work. There is a saying that *nothing breeds success like success itself*. The more information we can collect and share about the impact made by the partnership, the more willing the partners will be to continue to invest time and effort in future partnership activities. Portfolios could contain some of the following types of archives:

- The names of the key individuals responsible for the partnerships (including contact information)
- A statement of the goals and objectives of the partnership
- A description of the programs and activities sponsored by the partnership
- A record of the contributions of each of the partners (numbers of volunteers, training provided, mentors, equipment donated, etc.)
- Outcome measures (partnership pretests, posttests, attendance, test scores, grades, graduation rates, number of students going on to post–high-school training, etc.)
- Assessment of partnership goals and plans for future programs and activities
- Samples of student work (digital photos, video clips, student art work, etc.)

These portfolios can be in digital form and placed on the school website or copied to a CD and distributed to key stakeholders of the partnerships.

Parents and Families as Partners

There have been times when educators viewed families and parents as part of the problem, rather than a potential part of the solution. We have sometimes gotten caught up in the "blame game": blaming the lack of student success on the families that "haven't done their part in helping their children learn what the teachers were trying to teach." We have used traditional activities to seek to involve those families, and then we complain when they don't show up. Joyce Epstein (1995), in her landmark research, was able to identify six types of involvement that schools can offer families. This work was based on the idea that we should not expect all families to get involved in the same ways. Epstein's types of involvement include:

- *Parenting:* Assist families with parenting and child rearing, to provide an environment in the home that would prepare the child to enter school each day ready to learn.

♦ *Communicating:* Communicate with families about school programs and student progress with effective two-way communication.

♦ *Volunteering:* Parents can make significant contributions to the environment and functions of a school. Schools can get the most out of this process by creating flexible schedules, so more parents can participate, and by working to match the talents and interests of parents to the needs of students, teachers, and administrators.

♦ *Learning at Home:* Provide families with information about how to help their children with homework and learning-related activities.

♦ *Decision Making:* Include families as participants in school decisions and governance through PTA, school councils, committees, and other organizations.

♦ *Collaborating with the Community:* Provide coordination for the use of resources and services available to provide programs and services for families, students, and the school.

In the Community Learning Center you will find a comprehensive plan for engaging families. This plan will have programs and activities that address each of the six types of involvement identified by Epstein in her research. This will provide a variety of opportunities for different families who have a variety of differences. These differences come from some of the following conditions:

♦ The experiences of the parents with schools during their youth

♦ Level of educational attainment of parents

♦ Cultural orientations to schools and educators that were formed by in the countries of origin for many immigrant families

♦ Economic status that often determines where families are directing their priorities

♦ Work schedules and the number of jobs held by family members

Partnerships are proving to be more and more critical to student success. Educators are quickly learning that we desperately need to harness all the resources we can to support students as they strive for academic success.

References

Epstein, J. (1995, May). School/family/community partnerships. *Phi Delta Kappan*, 76(9):701-712.

Epstein, J. (2001). *School, family and community partnerships.* Boulder, CO: Westview Press.

National Association of Partners in Education (2002a). *Developing High-Quality After-School Partnership Programs.* Alexandria, VA: Author.

National Association of Partners in Education (2002b). *Partnerships 2000: A decade of growth and change.* Alexandria, VA: Author.

6

Collaboration for Improved Service Delivery

Journey into Community

The small conference room near the Community Learning Center office is filling up. It is the biweekly meeting of the Community Services Council. Representatives from social services, mental health, youth protective services, law enforcement, and the public health department; a counselor; and the director of the Community Learning Center are all at the meeting.

Each month a different agency representative facilitates the meetings. This month the meeting will be under the direction of the social service department representative who is assigned to the community served by the center. The police school liaison officer is going to serve as the recorder.

First on the agenda is the Jones family. They have two students enrolled in the center. The father is a disabled factory worker who is no longer able to work outside the home. The mother has worked at a variety of retail jobs but has been laid off for the past six weeks.

Several of the agencies represented in the meeting have had contact with the family in recent weeks. Social services is currently trying to find the family housing, as they are about to be evicted from their apartment. The police have been called to the home on several occasions for domestic disturbances. The teachers of the two brothers have seen a dramatic drop in their grades, attendance, and general behavior.

In the past, each of these agencies tended to work separately and independently with the family to address a part of the family's problem. Today's meeting represents a change in the way these agencies are working together to address the Jones family's needs.

Toward the end of the meeting, the discussion turned to how each agency might work in collaboration with the family to help provide a firm foundation for a positive environment for the children.

The Community Learning Center's Role

Some educators get nervous when talk turns to dealing with the socioeconomic needs of families. The cause of the nervousness is a fear that they will be expected to take on yet another role that will drain resources and energy away from their primary mission of educating children and youth. The conversation sometimes turns into a listing of the things that society has, over the years, shuffled off to the educational institutions, which were previously handled by families, churches, or other community agencies. That list often includes many of the tasks in the following list.

+ Providing a nutritious breakfast and lunch for children who live in low-income families

+ Teaching young people to drive automobiles

+ Developing character and values

+ Providing daycare services (often before and after school)

+ Sex education (politely called "family life education" in many schools)

+ Mentoring programs

+ Can you think of others that could be added to this list?

With these tasks serving as the background, we find ourselves in a society that is growing in complexity. Many families are experiencing stresses that we can't even begin to comprehend.

Slumping economies and demands for new workplace skills have put many of the family wage earners out of work. Drugs have become a plague on the lives of many family members, both children and parents. Poverty has brought the temptations of crime as a way to improve a way of life that knows only depravation. All these conditions that affect the lives of families show up in classrooms in communities across our country. Children take their seats with empty stomachs, minds blurred by drugs or filled with fear that they will be physically harmed when they leave the safety of the classroom.

The school or the Community Learning Center, working alone, cannot address all of these problems. It is going to take the efforts of all the resources of a whole community working together to address the needs and problems of today's families. There is no doubt that this effort is going to take some of the resources and attention of educators in the Community Learning Center. However, and this is crucial, if we do not become part of the solution to these problems, we will continue to face students who cannot experience any level of academic success because of the other issues they have to deal with in their lives. *Leave no child behind* becomes a useless political slogan if we cannot give each child the opportunity to participate in learning activities without the distractions of conditions in their lives that no one would wish for any child.

Joy Dryfoos (1994) in her book, *Full-Service Schools*, suggested that schools provide a home for a wide array of community services that serve children and their families. This idea fits comfortably with the Community Learning Center as long as it is clear that the services housed in the center are those that need to become more accessible for members of that particular community.

Questions to Consider in
Planning a Community Learning Center

**What school needs could be satisfied
through links with community partners?**

- ❏ Added learning experiences
- ❏ Volunteers and other resource staff
- ❏ Cost sharing
- ❏ Improved school image

**What are the major barriers to creating
the Community Learning Center?**

- ❏ Staff endorsement
- ❏ Program interrelationships and boundaries
- ❏ Arrangements for sharing space and equipment
- ❏ Administrative control
- ❏ Managerial arrangements
- ❏ Legal, liability, or financial requirements

Would public education programs be helped by:

- ❏ Closer relationships between educators and the public
- ❏ Expanded learning opportunities
- ❏ Improved communication with other segments of the community
- ❏ Use of the school for community purposes
- ❏ Conservation of limited education funding.

Source: U.S. Department of Education (1997, p. 18).

Community Health Clinics

Some communities have a real need to have greater access to health services. A community health clinic located in the Community Learning Center would bring those services closer to the people that need them. This might be especially true in rural communities that are located far from a hospital or doctor's office. At the same time, urban families may have other issues in acquiring needed health services. Lack of health insurance or the funds to pay for services often drive families to hospital emergency rooms, even for normal nonemergency procedures.

The National Health and Education Consortium (1995, p. 1) has proposed the establishment of health centers in public elementary schools.

> One of the public education's major challenges is coping with the health status—mental and physical—of its students and the impact of their health on their ability to learn. For decades educators and policy makers have discussed school and curriculum reform as vehicles for improving educational outcomes for our students. Increasingly, schools are acknowledging that education reform cannot occur without focusing on the other interrelated needs of families and children. Schools must commit themselves to both educating and helping build a foundation for learning.

The Consortium goes on to say that school health centers should be designed to help teachers teach by seeing that sick, hungry, or frightened students get the attention they need from qualified health experts, allowing these students to return to class ready to learn.

A health clinic with medical and dental services available to students and their families could be an important part of the mix of components located in some Community Learning Centers. Funding for this part of the center would not be the responsibility of the board of education. Other agencies and organizations that have the provision of healthcare as their mission can be involved in designing and operating the health clinic in the center. The programs and services offered by the clinic become a part of the services offered to the community through the center.

The staff of the health clinic can be a valuable asset for working with the many health-related issues that arise among the students in the center. Secondary schools need assistance for students who have become sexually active and risk the problems of sexually transmitted diseases and pregnancy. These issues carry the potential for controversy. Addressing these issues in a public setting like the Community Learning Center may disturb some community members. The reality is that teen pregnancy rates in many communities have skyrocketed in recent years. The numbers of children and teenagers who contract sexually transmitted diseases is also growing at alarming rates. Educators must join with healthcare professionals to address these problems. And the health clinic located in the Community Learning Center is one way of bringing those resources closer to those who need them.

Law Enforcement

In the 1970s, while I was in graduate school, I learned of a new program called the Police School Liaison Officer training program. Michigan State University was one of the lead institutions in the country in providing this training. The program prepared regular duty police officers for assignments in public schools. Their role was to be a connection between the school and law enforcement and to help provide a safe environment in the school building.

I can remember wondering why we would ever need police officers regularly assigned to a school building. We had not yet experienced the tragedy of Columbine High School, where students brought weapons to school and conducted an assault on fellow students and teachers that left several dead and wounded, and a nation in shock.

Today, even with statistics showing an overall decline in violence in schools, we are constantly reminded of the potential for tragic events that can strike any community. Communities are demanding that steps be taken to insure the safety of their children. Police officers in schools are not the oddity that they once were. They have become an accepted part of the team of professionals working in many schools. They handle issues of security in and around the building. They also work at establishing a relationship of trust with students that provides them with another person to turn to with problems.

Some of the issues that police school liaison officers can assist with are listed here.

- ♦ Deterring drug distribution and use on school grounds
- ♦ Gang activity
- ♦ Fighting and assaults
- ♦ Thefts
- ♦ Trespassers

The role of the law enforcement officer in the Community Learning Center can be extended to working with the community on issues of safety and security. Community Watch programs can be organized in which citizens keep an eye on neighborhoods for potential criminal activity. They could help homeowners and local businesses do security audits to make sure that they are as safe as possible.

Who Calls the Meeting?

A critical issue in many communities is who provides the energy to bring community agencies together in any kind of collaborative working relationship. While working at a community college in the Midwest, I was involved with another agency in trying to bring together a group of community service agencies to form a group to foster greater collaboration. It came to the point when we had to decide whose letterhead was going to be used to send out the invitation for the first meeting. That brought things to a screeching halt for several days. Finally, saner heads prevailed, and we got over the egos involved and sent out the invitation without using any agency letterhead.

The Community Learning Center can provide a great service to the community by providing the energy for bringing together community service agencies and organizations with children and families that need assistance. The center can also be the vehicle for these agencies and organizations to work together to make the best use of their resources.

Synergism

There is a term that began to show up in the conversations about interagency collaboration several years ago. The term is *synergism,* and it created quite a bit of confusion. Few of us had heard of it. Many times I have relied on a chemistry example to explain how synergism works. The dictionary definition involves the interaction of two or more agents or forces so that their combined effect is greater than the sum of their individual effects. Now, if you took two chemicals and ignited them individually with a flame and measured the heat given off, it might be 50 degrees from each. If you were to combine similar quantities of the two chemicals and ignite the mixture with a flame, the total heat given off might be 120 degrees. This represents a net gain of 20 degrees over the two chemicals working alone. What happens is that the properties of the two chemicals working together complement each other to create a greater energy output than when they worked alone.

Translating the chemistry example to agencies and organizations, we see that when two or more of them work together in a collaborative manner, their capacity to serve those in need is greater than if each of them worked alone.

Preventive Strategies to
Minimize Barriers to Collaboration

- Keep the commitment and activities simple at first. Move through each stage of developing the collaboration only when members are ready.

- Make clear communication a priority. Communicate with all members regularly, and avoid assuming that the members are informed on collaborative business.

- Spend time getting to know the other members. If most members do not know each other, schedule time for information sharing and team building at early meetings.

- When new members join the collaboration, make an extra effort to include them in the social and business activities of the group. People who are new often remember the little acts of courtesy and hospitality that helped them feel welcomed.

- Encourage members to be up-front about their needs. Set up win–win situations so that members' needs can be met whenever possible.

- Don't avoid turf issues and hidden agendas. Encourage negotiation and communication among member organizations that are in conflict. Bring in outside experts if necessary.

- Develop clear roles for members and leaders. Develop written statements that document commitments expected of participants.

- Plan activities that are fun. Celebrate the accomplishments of the collaboration. Recognize the contributions of the members and reward their accomplishments.

Source: The National Assembly of National Voluntary Health & Social Welfare Organizations (1997).

Collaboration can sometimes seem deceptively simple. It is hard to comprehend why something as simple as working together to better serve our common clientele, children and families, can be so difficult. Along with a score of other issues that affect the success of collaboration is the key issue of human relationships. One of my mentors, Jack Minzey, a national spokesperson for Community Education during the 1970s and 1980s, often said that we need to remember that "Agencies and organizations don't cooperate, but people do." We need to work hard at building the kind of relationship with professionals in other community-serving agencies that will support our working together. The changing cast of characters complicates this effort. We just get to a point where we have a great working relationship when someone in a key agency or organization gets transferred or promoted. That means that relationship building is an ongoing process that we must continue to maintain over the course of time.

Tips for Working with the Community Learning Center

- Involve teachers in needs assessment and planning from the beginning.

- Establish expectations for what and how materials will be shared.

- Where possible, integrate regular staff with collaborating agency or organization staff.

- Coordinate with teachers so that the program fills their needs and frees them to do more with their own class time.

- Establish a system for ongoing dialogue between school staff and collaborators to facilitate assessment, innovation, and the quick airing of grievances.

The Community Learning Center is committed to collaboration. Collaboration with community members, collaboration with service providers, and collaboration among the center staff. This statement is made with a full understanding of the investment that must be made to make collaboration work.

References

Dryfoos, J. G. (1994). *Full-service schools.* San Francisco: Jossey-Bass.

National Health and Education Consortium. (1995). *Putting children first: State level collaboration between education and health.* Washington, DC: Author.

The National Assembly of National Voluntary Health & Social Welfare Organizations (1997, 3rd printing). *The new community collaboration manual.* Washington, DC: Author.

U.S. Department of Education (1997). *Keeping schools open as community learning centers: Extending learning in a safe, drug-free environment before and after school.* Washington, DC: Author.

7

Afterschool Programs Connected to Student Success

Journey into Community

It is 4:30, and Principal Betty Larson stops by the family skills room to look in on "her kids." There are about a dozen kids anxiously hovering around stoves, watching intently. Today they are making hard candy, like the kind many adults used to get in their Christmas stockings. They are carefully recording temperature changes to make sure it reaches just the right stage to produce good candy. They will have weighed the contents both before and after the procedure to determine any loss of weight in the cooking process. These skills will be useful to them in their science classes the next day. These children are part of the Community Learning Center's Afterschool Adventure Club.

Down the hall there is a group of students in a computer lab working with a retired member of the community who lives just across the street. This volunteer knew nothing about computers until a year ago when he joined the Senior Computing Club, sponsored by the recreation department at the Community Learning Center. He got so excited about computers that he has taken two courses offered in the Center by the regional community college. He has learned enough to be very useful to the students who are busy working to get caught up on their assignments. He goes from student to student answering questions and sometimes just to give some friendly kidding about news of a budding romance.

There is also a group of girls who are working with mentors who come twice a week from a university located in the city. These mentors help with school studies but also serve as role models for these young ladies. Many of the kids have decided to go on to college because of the influence of their mentors.

Many communities have sponsored afterschool programs for kids for years and years. I can remember back to my own youth (even though I have to go back a good number of years) when my buddies and I spent hours involved in a variety of afterschool activities at the local YMCA and a Jewish Community Center near my home. Our community was a very ecumenical one, as you can see. These programs were outstanding, but in today's world, they would fall short in serving the vast number of children who need access to a safe and supportive environment. The schools I attended were closed at the end of the school day and did not to reopen until the next morning, when we all arrived for classes.

The community-based afterschool programs of my day had a capacity to serve only a small portion of the number of kids who lived in my community. This was a product of the limited facilities. Then there was the issue of cost. My parents were not wealthy; many times struggling to make ends meet in a tough postwar economy, but they made it a priority for the kids in our family to have access to the kinds of programs that would contribute to our later success in life. Many of the agencies running programs did have sliding scales for low-income families and scholarships to help out, but pride kept many families from accepting help.

Another drawback to those programs was the separation between the sponsoring agencies in the community and the schools. Little attempt was ever made to coordinate what was being done in community afterschool programs with what was being done in classrooms in the schools. One program was not able to support the other because there was often no communication between them.

After World War II, more women remained in the workforce, and a critical need emerged for childcare programs to bridge the gap between the time children got out of school and parents came home from work. The nation saw a steady growth in the number of childcare providers. These programs were widely varied in their sponsorship. Churches and not-for-profit agencies in the community developed many programs, and other programs were offered by privately run organizations that were operated for profit.

The many preschool programs that had been developed to provide daytime care for toddlers and infants while both parents were at work expanded their services to also provide afterschool childcare for school-aged children. My own children began in a preschool program and continued on in the afterschool program as they entered school.

The public schools of the country were not interested in providing (or not able to provide) the kind of afterschool programs that the public was seeking. In my own state of Virginia, public schools were prohibited from offering afterschool program in school buildings. State law regulated this until the early 1980s.

Before the law was changed, my university, Virginia Tech, partnered with the University of Virginia (UVA) to sponsor a conference for public school Community Educators to examine the prospects of schools becoming the home for quality afterschool programs. This was triggered by the fact that there were not enough quality childcare facilities that were offering programs for school-aged children.

Larry Decker, the Director of the Mid-Atlantic Center for Community Education at UVA, and I were the chief architects of the conference. We had arranged to bring several experts in afterschool programming from out of the state. The conference attracted nearly 100 people and got off to a surprisingly rocky start. Right off the bat, we discovered that in the audience were several representatives of the private, for-profit network of preschool programs in the state. These private providers saw this conference as a move to put them out of business. They felt that the public schools, with their tax-supported facilities and access to students, would provide unfair competition and rob them of income.

Our position was that the need for quality afterschool childcare was so great in our state that it was going to take the efforts of all of our public and private resources to meet it. We also felt that public schools should be encouraged to explore partnerships with private providers to offer afterschool programs. Contracts could be drawn to allow private providers to use school facilities to provide programs at the end of the normal school day and on teacher workdays when the students would not be in classes. After considerable dialogue on both sides, we were able to complete the rest of the conference program.

Soon after that conference, the state changed the law to allow schools to become involved in afterschool programs. And many communities saw new partnerships formed with private providers to use school facilities to serve children. But, as the 20th century wound down, we saw the need for afterschool programs once more back in the spotlight. Without much in the way of public support, the existing network of afterschool programs was still falling short of reaching all children. We found school-aged children, especially in low-income communities, left to fend for themselves in the afternoon between the time school let out and parents got home. The media labeled these children "latchkey kids." High-risk behaviors among these children from the hours of 2:30 to 6 P.M. rose at alarming rates.

What do kids do afterschool?

- Juvenile crime triples from 3 to 8 P.M. and peaks from 3 to 4 P.M. during the afterschool hours.
- In the United States, 28 percent of all children live with a single working parent or two working parents.
- Between 5 and 7 million (possibly as many as 15 million) latchkey children are home alone after school.
- The most common activity for children after school is watching TV—on average 23 hours a week.

What do afterschool programs do for kids?

Children who regularly attend quality programs have:

- Better grades and conduct in school
- Better peer relations and emotional adjustment
- More academic and enrichment opportunities
- Students who spend one to four hours per week in extracurricular activities are 49 percent less likely to use drugs and 37 percent less likely to become teen parents.

For example, students who attend the Anchorage Alaska afterschool program:

- Have made academic gains
- Are feeling safer
- Are turning in their homework more often
- Like school more
- More than 1,500 K–8 students were involved in afterschool activities at 17 Community Learning Center sites.

Source: Anchorage, Alaska, website, http://www.asdk12.org/depts/community_ed/cclc.asp

The administration of President Bill Clinton responded to concerns about the lack of quality afterschool childcare and lifelong learning opportunities for adults by supporting legislation to create Community Learning Centers in schools across the United States. These centers were to transform traditional schools into a place where children and young people would be able to have access to high-quality afterschool programs, adults would find access to programs that would address their educational needs, buildings would be available for community use, and community agencies serving children and families would work in collaboration to provide needed services.

The original intent of the program is described in a grant application publication released by the U.S. Department of Education (2001, p. 1):

> 21st Century Community Learning Centers enable school districts to fund public schools as community education centers keeping children safe in the afterschool hours and providing academic enrichment, homework centers and tutors, and a range of cultural, developmental and recreational opportunities. *In addition, lifelong learning activities are available for community members in local school settings* [emphasis added]. School-based 21st Century Learning Centers, established around the country, are providing safe, drug-free, supervised, and cost-effective afterschool, weekend, and summer havens for children, youth, and their families.

When it came time to seek congressional appropriations for this vision of Community Learning Centers, it became an issue of finding a middle ground that would attract support from both liberal and conservative political factions. Afterschool programs provided that politically safe middle ground. Little attention has been paid to making lifelong learning activities and other services for the community available in the centers.

In a recent study at Harvard University, Hall (2002, p. 3) concluded that, "Yet despite this apparent support for expanding learning opportunities for the entire community, implementation of the 21st CCLC Act has looked very different: It has created few new educational opportunities for adults." Hall's study is one of the first to raise questions about the fulfillment of the original broad intent of the legislation. In most cases, schools are not becoming Community Learning Centers as a result of the funding that has been allocated for the 21st CCLC Act.

Appropriations for the program, which began in fiscal year 1995, have climbed from just over $100 million to $1 billion in 2002 (the bill was authorized at $1.5 billion, but not fully funded). In 2002 over 6,800 schools in 1,597 communities sponsored Community Learning Center programs, serving thousands of children and youth. Funding to this point has been limited to rural and inner-city urban schools that can document that they are serving a population of students who would be classified as high-risk in terms of educational failure.

With funding for the 2002–2003 fiscal year, the responsibility for the distribution of funds for the 21st Century Community Learning Centers moved from the federal government to the states. Each state was charged with establishing a plan for how funds would be distributed and how the program was to be operated. In addition to this change, the eligibility for funding was expanded to make wider inclusion of community-based organizations. These organizations are required to maintain a strong academic enrichment component in order to receive funding. States are also required to restrict funding to programs and services that were limited to the students and members of their families. The dimension of lifelong learning for adult community members has been lost.

Talking about Afterschool

"You can probably think of a thousand ways to spend $2.2 million, and much of what you'd buy would probably be greatly devalued, if not worthless, after a few years. This week I have seen how the Fort Worth school district and the city of Fort Worth have been spending that amount of money, and I can't think of a better way, or a more profitable way, to use it . . . . After visiting a few afterschool programs financed with tax dollars, I have no doubt that we're getting more than our money's worth . . . . The program was designed to provide a safe place for students regarded as latchkey kids, youngsters who otherwise would be at home unsupervised by an adult after school . . . . More than 3,700 students districtwide are involved in this hugely successful program, but if there is one thing bad about it, it's that only slightly more than half of the elementary campuses can participate. Why don't we double the money allocated and at least provide this opportunity at all 74 elementary campuses, and most of the middle schools? Imagine spending money that helps children learn, develops their character, expands their horizons and keeps them safe, all while they are having fun."

Source: Columnist Bob Ray Sanders, Fort Worth Star Telegram, March 8, 2002

Connecting Afterschool to School

A fifth grader participating in an inner-city afterschool program was overheard to say, "I wish school was like afterschool." Now that could be interpreted as a vote for the snacks that are served, the recreational opportunities that are offered, or the way the learning is made to be a fun activity.

Afterschool programs have the opportunity to create learning activities that are fun, but yet activities that are connected to what is going on in the regular-day classrooms. This will provide students who need some extra help learning in specific content areas the chance to catch up and draw even with their classmates. It also offers students who are up to speed in a certain content areas the chance to extend their learning or focus on another area where they may need help.

Quality afterschool programs are highly connected with the regular-day program instruction and curriculum, but they don't duplicate what goes on in classrooms during the day. They do offer interactive activities that focus on acquiring skills, problem solving, and exposure to new experiences. They also provide for many kids a badly needed connection with caring adults. This is made possible by situations that are created after school where there is time for adults to interact with students in more depth than time allows during the regular school day.

All of this doesn't just happen. It takes a great deal of communication and collaboration between the regular-day classroom teachers and the afterschool program staff. It requires that individual students who are falling behind be identified so that they can be provided with the right kind of help in the afterschool program.

Communities Meeting
the Need for Afterschool Activities

Children's Aid Society Community Schools New York City, NY. Contact: C. Warren Moses, 212–949–4921.

When I.S. 218 in New York City decided to become a Community Learning Center, the school created an afterschool program with the help of the Children's Aid Society and other community partners. A parent survey indicated concern about homework, so the afterschool program initially focused on providing homework assistance. Within months, two computer labs, dance classes, arts and crafts, band, and some entrepreneurial programs were added to the afterschool program, with learning and homework always central. The afterschool program gradually evolved into an extended-day program in which, for example, non–English-speaking children can attend Project Advance for special instruction in Spanish and English as a second language.

Evaluations show that the afterschool program at I.S. 218 positively affected both the school and the children. When compared to a school with similar characteristics, I.S. 218 students performed, on average, 15 percent higher on reading and math exams. These results can be attributed, in part, to the afterschool activities provided to all students.

One of the many fantastic tools presented in *Beyond the Bell: A toolkit for creating effective afterschool programs* (Walters, Caplan, & McElvain, 2000, p. 52) is a form to conduct a survey of teacher programming needs. Directions to teachers state,

> In order to plan effective afterschool programs that support the regular school day, we are asking teachers to list the subjects or topics areas where students need additional assistance. Your suggestions should be based on assessments of student achievement, observations, student preferences, or parent feedback. For each subject or topic area, please list specific skills where students need assistance and assign a priority level—low, medium, or high—to these skills.

The data from the survey are used to drive planing for afterschool programs and services for students.

How Does It Work?

A great deal of attention needs to be paid to making the collaboration between the afterschool and regular-day school program work. The authors of *Beyond the Bell* (Walters, Caplan, & McElvain, 2000, p. 61) have stated the challenges of this task very articulately. "A culture of integration depends on building trust, understanding, mutual respect, and common purpose between school and afterschool staff. It cannot be forced through persuasion, logic, or policies."

There needs to be regular opportunities for communication between teachers and afterschool program staff. In some communities this is facilitated by the active involvement of day classroom teachers in afterschool programs. This involvement takes on different forms in different Community Learning Centers. Some teachers volunteer to spend some time each week to work with their students in afterschool programs, and others do this on a paid basis. While making visits to several centers, I was concerned about teachers getting burned out or too physically tired at the end of the regular school day to participate in afterschool programs. But the response I got from those teachers surprised me. They said that they found the opportunity to interact with their students in a more relaxed atmosphere, and to see the progress they were making, to be an invigorating experience. Rather than being worn out when they left school, they reported going home on a high note.

There are always going to be issues to resolve. Issues like sharing space and equipment, scheduling activities, and who is responsible for what. These and host of others that can arise are solvable if attention has been paid to establishing a culture of integration built on trust, understanding, mutual respect, and common purpose. At some point the experience of having a seamless program for kids could emerge. Getting rid of the terms *regular-day* and *afterschool* would be useful in attaining a goal of having a seamless program. Perhaps if we considered the school day as extending from an early morning hour until when the last student departs for home, then we could eliminate those distinctions that have been distractions in the past.

Common Elements
of Quality Afterschool Programs

Researchers and practitioners have identified some common elements found in high-quality programs. The elements are important in meeting the needs of the diverse population of children and youth that are part of our communities. The common elements of quality afterschool program include:

- Goal driven with strong management
- Plan for long-term sustainability in place
- Quality staffing
- Attention to safety, health, and nutrition issues
- Effective partnerships
- Strong involvement of families
- Extended learning opportunities
- Linkages between school-day and afterschool personnel
- Evaluation of program progress and effectiveness

A Resource Guide for Planning and Operating Afterschool Programs has been produced by the Southwest Educational Development Laboratory (Bagby, 2001). This guide provides a listing of resources in the areas of management, communication, programming, integrating K–12 and afterschool, community building and collaboration, and education. The guide is available free of charge as a PDF file on the SEDL website at http://www.sedl.org/pubs/fam18/afterschool.pdf.

Afterschool Impact

"The impact of afterschool programs is tangible, quantifiable and wide-reaching. A growing body of research shows that participation in afterschool programming not only promotes real learning, but also reduces involvement in high-risk activities and curbs juvenile crime. Parents seem to understand these benefits of afterschool programs, and they are clamoring for more. A recent survey conducted by Massachusetts 2020 revealed that the parents of roughly 520,000 school-age children want their child to participate more in afterschool programs. We call on the state to seize the opportunity to deepen its commitment to education reform by more systematically supporting learning opportunities for children that extend beyond the school day. The need is clearly there. It is now up to the state, in partnership with the private sector, community-based organizations and families, to meet that need in serious and thoughtful ways."

Source: Op-Ed piece by Jennifer Davis, President of Massachusetts 2020, and S. Paul Reville, Executive Director of the Pew Forum on Standards-Based Reform at Harvard University, in the *Worcester Telegram & Gazette*, March 7, 2002

Partnerships Make a Difference

A fundamental principle of Community Education is that the *schools cannot do it all by acting alone*. To make any program work in the Community Learning Center, it is important to establish strong partnerships with agencies, businesses, and organizations with resources that can have a positive impact on kids. I had the opportunity to visit Mobile, Alabama, a few years ago and was impressed by the level of partnerships that they have developed. The following is an excerpt from *The Extended-Day News*, which is published by the Alabama Department of Education in collaboration with the Alabama Cooperative Extension Service and the Alabama Department of Human Resources (Zoghby, 2001, p. 15).

> The Mobile County Public School System has had long-standing partnerships with the Boys and Girls Clubs of South Alabama, Inc., and the Alabama Cooperative Extension System. This past school year and summer, this partnership provided new services for eight afterschool programs which were partially funded through the Dependent Care Development Grant. Two programs continue through September in rural middle schools. Programs were conducted in three elementary schools and five middle schools. Both urban and rural schools participated. . . .
>
> The programs included the Boys and Girls Clubs' *Power Hour* homework help; age-appropriate life skills, such as *Talking with T.J.*, a 4-H program that teaches young children (Grades 2–4) how to get along and be able to accomplish tasks in a group; *Smart Moves*, a Boys and Girls Club of America, Inc. skill development program that focuses on self-awareness, decision-making and interpersonal skills, while communicating age-appropriate information about alcohol and other drugs; and Growing *Strong*, an Extension System gardening program designed to use the garden as a tool for learning. Parents were also involved in after-hours

events in two middle schools where they partici-
pated in a special *Principles of Parenting* Program at
two middle schools. One of the middle schools offered special remedial assistance through the
Lightspan Achieve Now Program, a nationally recognized program designed to improve basic skills.
These programs were included in curriculum that
included the arts, recreation, field trips, summer
camp activities, and community service. The Alabama Cooperative Extension System provides staff
training and curriculum for the programs. The Dependent Care grants coupled with other funding
sources such as United Way and federal, state, and
local government funds provided Mobile with
eight unique school-based programs. The programs were conducted Monday through Friday
during the schools year and the summer, with
approximately 1,000 children participating.

It is plain to see that Mobile has worked hard at forming
effective partnerships that are working to sustain a fine
afterschool program that will be around in the years to come.
Sustainability has been a major concern for communities that
have been recipients of 21st Century Community Learning
Center grants. One of the keys to sustainability is the success
in engaging a wide range of partners in the effort. Where there
are strong partnerships, there will be resources found to continue to serve the needs of the children of the community.

The Afterschool Alliance

The Afterschool Alliance is a nonprofit organization dedicated to raising awareness of the importance of afterschool programs and advocating for quality, affordable programs for all children. It is supported by a group of public, private, and nonprofit organizations that share the Alliance's vision of ensuring that all children have access to afterschool programs by 2010.

The Alliance provides access to critical research in the field of afterschool programs and provides a voice of nationwide voice of advocacy. The Alliance is credited with coining the phrase "Afterschool for All" to commemorate their goal of having a quality afterschool program accessible for every student in the country. Its website is http://www.afterschoolalliance.org.

References

Bagby, J. H. (2001). *A resource guide for planning and operating afterschool programs.* Austin, TX: Southwest Educational Development Laboratory.

Davis, J., & Reville, S. P. (2002, March 7). Afterschool impact. *Worcester Telegram & Gazette,* 2002.

Hall, M. E. (2002). *From community school to afterschool: Examining the implementation of the 21st century community learning centers act.* Unpublished thesis, Boston: Harvard University.

Sanders, B. R. (2002). Talking about afterschool. *Fort Worth Star Telegram.*

U.S. Department of Education. (2001). *21st century community learning centers program: Application for grants.* CFDA #84.287. Washington, DC: Author.

Walters, K. E., Caplan, J. G., & McElvain, C. K. (2000). *Beyond the bell: A toolkit for creating effective afterschool programs.* Oak Brook, IL: North Central Regional Educational Laboratory.

Zoghby, M. (2001, Fall). Mobile County–Boys and Girls Clubs… Youth-serving organizations. *The Extended-Day News*, Alabama Department of Education.

8

Making Technology Work for Students and Community

Journey into Community

It is early Saturday morning on a gloomy winter day. The Community Learning Center is beginning to fill up with kids and their parents. They are here for a variety of reasons. One family is here to participate in the "Kids Teach" program, in which the parents learn what the students have been learning in the past few weeks. Using computers in the center, the kids can take their parents through the various learning activities they have been doing. They also show off work products that are posted on their personal websites.

Down the hall a group of senior citizens from the community are getting their first-ever chance to learn how to use a computer to explore the Internet and send email to grandchildren located in cities far away. Earlier in the week there were evening classes for a group of single moms who want to obtain job skills in the computer technology area.

Teachers have access to technology tools that allow them to bring resources from around the world into their classrooms. They can take students on a virtual tour of the famous Louvre Art Museum in Paris, access library materials in many of the world's great libraries, and use the Internet to present student work products to members of the community. Technology is not viewed as an *add-on*, but it is integrated into the total instructional process.

The technology of the Community Learning Center is treated like a gym or other facility that is made available to members of the community to use as much as is practically possible. This access is helping to close the gap between students who have computers in their homes and those who don't.

Unlocking the Technology

Many of us have been brought up in an age where technology held a certain mystical power. We have seen computers evolve from the size of large air-conditioned rooms to lightweight laptops. These new, small computers have a hundred times or more the computing capabilities of those early huge computers. But, with all the changes that have taken place, one thing that has not changed for many of us is the way we think about technology.

We have decided in our heads that technology is so fragile that it can break at any minute. The truth is that we are surrounded by various technology applications every day in our lives, and it rarely lets us down. That doesn't mean that we don't occasionally forget our passwords or forget just how we are suppose to find that document we stored on our computer. What we need to remember is that the technology we have in today's Community Learning Center will become obsolete faster than it will break or wear out.

We have to use the Community Learning Center to unlock the technology that has been kept away from many families in our communities. Even with the price of home computer falling below the $700 range, it is hard for a family living close to the poverty line to justify spending that kind of money.

I often tell the story of a local school superintendent who came to talk to one of my classes about the challenges that schools will face in the future. He talked about how his 3-year-old son could go into his office at home, boot up one of the two computers they have, and log on to the Internet. He expressed concern about sending his son to a kindergarten that used no computers in the classroom. After class I told him that I remembered driving down the road to his house and passing a trailer court. I told him that I would be willing to wager a considerable sum that a child will leave one of those trailer homes to get on the school bus with his son. And that child will leave behind, not a home with a computer with high-speed Internet access, but a home with barely any printed matter suitable for him to read. That is what is now being called the *digital divide*. We must not ignore the impact of the disparity that is created in how children enter school ready or not ready to learn. We also cannot ignore the disparity that is created when children do homework without the benefit of access to technology in their homes.

The data in the following chart shows what a range exists between households in different income brackets and in households of different race and ethnic backgrounds. The percentage of households with computers goes up rapidly as the income of the households increases. There are also significant differences in households when sorted by race and ethnic origin.

Figure 8.1. Percentage of U.S. Households With a Computer By Income, Race/Hispanic Origin, 2000

Race/ Ethnicity	Under $15,000	$15,000– $34,999	$35,000- $74,999	$75,000+
White	22.8	40.8	68.7	87.0
Black	11.5	27.3	52.7	83.4
Asian American & Pacific Island	39.4	53.5	72.4	86.9
Hispanic	12.5	27.8	55.9	76.1

Source: U.S. Dept. of Commerce, National Telecommunication and Information Administration, October 2000.

One way of addressing this problem is to use the Community Learning Center to unlock technology for many of the members of the community who have not had access in the past. Public libraries in many communities are models for how that can happen. Publicly accessible computer workstations are now appearing in libraries across the country. Trained staff are available to assist people in using the computers to complete various tasks ranging from surfing the Internet to preparing résumés. There are often waiting lists of people who are in line to use a computer. Classes are often provided to help community members learn new computer skills. The Community Learning Center can complement the work of libraries and other agencies in making more technology available to meet the demands of the community.

Using Community Expertise

Maybe it is because I currently live in an area that is home to many of the major technology corporations in the country, but it seems to me that we are not making the best use of the resources in our communities when it comes to technology. It is no secret that business applications of technology lead those made by educational institutions by a long way. Most computers available for use in many schools today are at least one or two generations behind those at use in the business world. In the past, educators have been guilty of being satisfied with soliciting their business partners for their cast-off computer hardware. Although that was helpful, we often missed the most important resource that we could use: the technology expertise in those businesses, that is, the people resources, not hardware.

On a recent visit to the headquarters office of Booz, Allen, Hamilton, Inc., an international management consulting company, I was invited to visit the "toyshop." Not knowing what to expect, I found a workshop filled wall-to-wall with the very latest innovations in technology. The company obtains the latest in technology from vendors around the world and asks its employees to spend time "playing" with these new tools to see what kind of applications might be made by their clients.

The Community Learning Center needs to find partners in their communities that are willing to assist in examining new technologies and how they might be applied to support teaching and learning. These partners can also provide training to teachers and staff on how to use technology tools more effectively. They often can make seats available to educators in training programs that are being provided for their own staff, or help in developing training specifically designed for teachers and administrators.

Important Resource

There are many useful resources available to assist the Community Learning Center in planning for the effective use of technology. One that stands out is the Community Technology Centers' Network (CTCN). This organization envisions a society "in which all people are equitably empowered by technology skills and usage" (http://www.ctcnet.org/mission.html/). They are a leading advocate of equitable access to computers and related technologies. They are active in encouraging partnerships and collaborations that offer resources to bring about "universal technological enfranchisement."

This organization provides a startup manual that gives excellent directions for developing a Community Technology Center (CTC). This manual is available at no charge on their website. The concept of the CTC is very consistent with the mission of the Community Learning Center, and it provides an excellent approach to making technology available to all members of the community. Community Technology Centers are currently located in a wide variety of institutions and organizations, such as community centers, schools, Boys and Girls Clubs, and libraries. The Community Learning Center is a natural location for a CTC.

The startup manual offers some basic steps to be taken in developing a CTC. The process for starting a new CTC is very close to a process that could be used in establishing a Community Learning Center.

How a CTC is Created

- Form a CTC Steering Committee to serve as the governing body for the CTC or as an advisory committee to the agency's existing governance structure.

- Engage in a process of community mapping to identify interests and needs of prospective participants along with assets and strengths available through other community enterprises and community members themselves.

- Form partnerships and develop commitments for assistance from members of the community (e.g., space, volunteers, funding, equipment, and furnishings).

- Research and structure program offerings in response to identified needs and interests (e.g., adult education, afterschool sessions, job preparation, elder services, and family and preschool programs).

- Initiate a pilot program through which to test the planned programming structure and to further refine conclusions relating to community interest and need.

- Consider and plan for the operational needs of the CTC (e.g., space, hardware, software, personnel, and resulting financial requirements).

- Develop a business plan mapping the CTC's operational and financial assumptions so that interested parties and donors can buy into the effort.

- Engage in whatever additional fund-raising, space and equipment acquisition, or staff and volunteer recruitment is necessary to make the plan operational. Do not plan to start full operations until the steering committee is satisfied that the CTC has sufficient backing to stay in operation for at least 12 months.

Source:
Stone, 2000, http://www.ctcnet.org/mission.html/

A Research Base
for Technology in the Center

There is a lot we can learn from research about the role of technology in the Community Learning Center. White, Ringstaff, and Kelley (2002) reviewed research studies on the benefits of computer-based technology in education. Based on their review, they developed a set of elements that need to be part of the planning process for technology in the Community Learning Center.

Considerations for Technology Planning
in the Community Learning Center

- Match technology with goals.

- Include technology as one piece of the puzzle.

- Provide adequate and appropriate professional development.

- Change teacher beliefs about learning and teaching.

- Provide sufficient equipment for adequate computer-to-student ratio.

- Make equipment accessible, in classrooms rather than computer labs.

- Consider computer access at home.

- Plan for the long term.

- Provide technical and instructional support.

- Integrate technology within the curricular framework.

Source: White, Ringstaff, and Kelley (2002, pp. 2–3)

Closing Thoughts on Technology

We need to be careful not to look at technology as a panacea for the challenges we face in providing quality education for all members of our community. However, technology offers great potential for enhancing the mission of the Community Learning Center in every community. We know that technology can facilitate learning for children as well as adults. It should be viewed as an important tool in the teaching and learning process. The Community Learning Center can play an important role in making technology more accessible for all members of the community and work to eliminate the digital divide that exists in our society.

References

Stone, A. (2000). *Center start-up manual.* Cambridge, MA: Community Technology Centers' Network.

U.S. Department of Commerce, National Telecommunications and Information Administration. (2000). *Falling through the net: Toward digital inclusion.* Washington, D.C. p 113.

White, N., Ringstaff, C., & Kelley, L. (2002). *Getting the most from technology in schools—Knowledge brief.* San Francisco: West Ed.

9

Shared Decision Making, Shared Accountability

Journey into Community

The cartoon character Pogo says, "None of us are as smart as all of us." That goes a long way to describe how this Community Learning Center functions. The Steering Council's monthly meeting is about to get started. It is 6 P.M., and there is a light meal being served. Meetings used to be held in the afternoon hours, but few of the community members who were on the council were ever able to attend. The teachers on the council agreed to try having the meeting in the early evening on a trial basis. That was four months ago, and everyone agrees now that it was the right thing to do.

Serving the meal tonight are two students who are also members of the council. They are serving, because it is their turn on a rotating basis. Next month one of them will take on the role of group facilitator. When they first joined the group, they would not have dreamed that they would one day be in charge of facilitating the whole meeting. They are confident enough now because of participation in several training workshops. In the workshops everyone was given a chance to practice leadership skills that are now being used in the group. All the members of the group rotate through the facilitator and recorder roles.

The major topics of the meeting tonight are a review of the data that have been collected to evaluate the impact of a new mentoring program, a proposal to make a new program to make dental services more available to children and families, and a report of a committee that was formed to address some serious pedestrian safety issues in the community. Much of the work of the council is done by an active set of committees and task forces.

It is popular today to advocate *site-based management* and *shared decision making* in schools. Unfortunately, it must be easier to talk about than to actually do it. Many school boards have mandated that schools institute some form of management that would extend involvement in decision making to the school building level. Teachers have greeted those announcements with some excitement and a lot of skepticism. That skepticism was built on years of experience in schools where teachers were generally powerless to influence issues important to how schools were organized, how students were treated, and what was taught.

Decision Making in
Prince William County (VA) Public Schools

In a statement of the culture or common set of beliefs for their schools you can find "a belief that decision-making is best accomplished through a collaborative process." They go on to specify that "each school and central department will develop long-range plans that include a statement of mission, goals, performance standards, objectives, and action plans. The plans will be developed through a collaborative partnership among school staff, parents, students, and the community." Each school is required to have an advisory council made up of teachers, staff, and members of the community. This council is a key component in the planning that is done at the building level. (Policies can be viewed at http://www.pwcs.edu/admin/qmp.pdf.)

The Prince William County schools have won many awards for their procedures for involving the community. In 2001 *Time* magazine selected Stonewall Jackson High School as its high school of the year. The article announcing the award (Winters, 2001) cited the school's use of technology to involve parents in their children's education and decision making in the school.

Principals are often not so opposed to involving teachers, parents, and community members in school decision making as they sometimes appear. Many of them understand the value in getting teachers and the community to develop a sense of ownership in their school. The reservation that many of them have is based on the accountability system that school districts have had in place for years.

That accountability system tends to focus on principals being held individually responsible for the outcomes of the schools they lead. Principals have told me that they would be more inclined to share the power of making decision if their jobs were not on the line each year when the results of standardized tests are reported for each school.

They tell of annual visits to the superintendent's office to review how well the students in their school have done during the past year. Some are even being threatened with being removed from their jobs if the performance of their students doesn't improve. A principal in a medium size suburban school in Massachusetts had this to say about shared decision making:

> The state-mandated governance group is supposed to have decision-making power; but since I'm responsible and accountable for this school, I reserve the final decisions for myself. (Webster, 1994, p. 71)

My recommendation to these principals is that when they are invited to the superintendent's office for their annual review, they should take their site-based councils with them. If there are any objections, they should tell their superintendent that if they are going to share the power to make decisions, then those who are involved in making those decisions should also share in the accountability for the results. We have to resolve the disconnect between school districts wanting to have shared decision making in their schools but not changing the system of accountability. Accountability needs to be tied to those who had a role in making those decisions. This is the only way that we will ultimately be able to effectively involve a wide range of stakeholders in the process of deciding how their Community Learning Centers should be operated.

Preparing Decision Makers

One mistake commonly made by school districts in their attempt to implement shared decision making at the school site is the lack of commitment to providing training for all those who will be involved in the decision-making process. Too often it is just assumed that all you have to put in place are the structures for involvement. School councils are carefully organized with a mandate to bring together a representative group of stakeholders, and then they are expected to meet and begin functioning as an effective team. Most teachers and principals have not had training in what needs to take place for a group to be effective in decision making. And often, even fewer community members have had such training. What little training is provided for members of school councils is usually limited to presentations on policies describing what they can and cannot do as a council.

Setting the Agenda for the Future

School councils should be charged with establishing a vision for the future. That vision needs to be a product of widespread involvement on the part of the school community stakeholders. A few years ago, while writing *Transforming Schools into Community Learning Centers,* I frequently referred to *stakeholders*. The spell checker in my computer kept telling me that there was no such word. This is not the case today; we find that the term has come into common use to describe those who have the most to lose or gain by events that take place in the system where they reside. In this case, where they reside is in the community that serves as home to the Community Learning Center.

Stakeholders could be used interchangeably with the corporate term *stockholder,* since there is implied ownership that comes with the definition. We need all who are part of the community to feel ownership of the agenda that drives the programs, services, and activities that take place in the Community Learning Center.

Beyond the Bell (Walters, Caplan, & McElvain, pp. 1–2), which has become the bible for those who are developing afterschool programs, identifies some key components that should guide the decisions of all programs. These key components have a lot of relevancy for how the Community Learning Center operates.

- ◆ Think strategically. The vision for the future of the program should shape every decision.
- ◆ Think inclusively. The program belongs to the community. Therefore, members of the community should have a voice in, and responsibility for, its operation.
- ◆ Think collaboratively. Programs should reflect the interdependence of a community through the sharing of ideas, mission, and resources. Coordinators can foster this interaction by considering partnership with those who offer it, seeking partnership with those who might offer it, and eliciting partnership from those who should offer it.

Creating a Shared Vision

All agenda building needs to start with a vision of the future that is shared by all of the stakeholders. The National Center for Community Education has developed the Five-Step Visioning Process that has been used with thousands of 21st Century Community Learning Center grantees.

The Five-Step Visioning Process

Step 1: Visioning—What is our vision of where the program will be in X years?

Step 2: Identifying the Challenges—What are the challenges or barriers to achieve this vision?

Step 3: Prioritizing the challenges—Of these challenges, which are the five most important?

Step 4: Identifying needs and assets—What needs will affect our ability to address these challenges? What resources or assets are available to help address these challenges?

Step 5: Strategizing—Given our needs and assets, what strategies could we use to address the challenges?

(This process, including worksheets, is available from the National Center for Community Education, *21st Century Visioning The Planning Process Workbook*. Available online at www.nccenet.org.)

The Five-Step Visioning Process is one that needs to be used inclusively. If it were implemented as a staff planning process, it would lose the power of diversity in the ideas represented around the table and fail to develop a sense of ownership among stakeholders in the community.

How Leadership Groups Develop

Group development in any situation is much like a marriage. There is a process that the group must go through to reach a level of maturity that allows them to function effectively as a group. In marriage there is courtship, which is analogous to people being recruited, elected, or selected to participate in a group that will provide guidance to the Community Learning Center.

The next phase, and a highly important one, is the honeymoon. Mohr and Dichter (2001, p. 745) share a rich description through the words of a teacher.

This is terrific! Finally, I am a part of a group that meets with the leader. I feel valued; my voice is being heard. I am still not comfortable disagreeing with the group, especially publicly, but it's exciting to feel that we will be able to make a real change.

Groups typically go from the honeymoon to a phase of conflict. Some group dynamics theorists call this the *storming* stage. The members of the group begin to feel comfortable enough with each other to begin to question how things are being decided and perhaps what is not being decided. There is often frustration about the lack of progress or the lack of substance. There is sometimes a temptation to withdraw and just let someone else make the decisions, "like the way it used to be done."

With the proper support and training, the group can work through the early phases of frustration to deal with issues like, "How can we improve our teamwork?" Or, "How can we make better use of our time?" Groups then enter into a phase of maturity where a learning community begins to emerge.

That mature-group phase is described by the words that a teacher might use to describe it.

Finally, we're proactive and make our own agenda rather than reacting to those of others. We've also learned to be inclusive; we avoid us/them scenarios. We rarely make decisions before we have enough knowledge, and we make better decisions because they include more points of view. ... And, we're all taking responsibility for making sure that [raising standards] happens, we've stopped pointing the mental finger at one another. (Mohr & Dichter, 2001, p. 747)

The words of the teacher in the quote provide a compelling argument for collaborative decision making. The Community Learning Center, which has inclusive collaboration as key part of its culture, would need to invest heavily in establishing a process for involving a wide range of stakeholders in the decisions of the center. That investment would include training for members of decision-making group. Training would need to include how to work more effectively as a group.

Group Roles

The roles presented next have been developed and tested with a variety of groups over time. The roles are *facilitator, recorder,* and *member.* When applied on a regular basis, they produce better meetings and allow the group to function more effectively. The roles also become second nature to the group as they become more comfortable in performing the roles. The recommendation to rotate the roles of facilitator and recorder is two-fold. First, persons in those roles need to limit their participation in the discussion of the group and focus on helping the group process to flow smoothly. It would be unfair to eliminate the same members at each meeting. Rotating helps to share this responsibility and allows everyone the opportunity to serve in those roles and still have a chance to participate. The second reason for the rotation is to allow group members to practice and improve their leadership skills. The outcome that is almost universally experienced by groups using these roles is increased ownership and commitment on the part of the members.

When group membership is small (four to eight people), it is advisable to allow the facilitator and recorder to participate in the discussion of the group. They must also be attentive to their roles. In larger groups, if the recorder and facilitator are compelled to participate in the discussion, they can hand off their responsibilities to another until they have made their contribution to the discussion. Then they can resume their role serving the group.

Group Leadership Roles
in the Community Learning Centers

Shared decision making means the commitment of long hours meeting with stakeholders to determine a vision, develop a plan, and assess results. To make this process more effective, the following group roles are recommended.

Facilitator (a rotating role)

- Neutral servant of the group
- Focuses the group on the common task
- Doesn't evaluate or contribute ideas
- Suggests alternative procedures or methods when the group is stuck
- Encourages everyone to participate
- Helps the group to find win–win situations

Recorder (a rotating role)

- Maintains group memory and public record
- Accurately records essence of ideas from the group
- Checks with the group for accuracy and asks for feedback
- Supports facilitator
- Uses a variety of techniques to highlight ideas and information

Member (everybody)

- Keep the facilitator neutral
- Keep an eye on the group memory for accuracy
- Concentrate on the content
- Contribute ideas
- Listen, Listen, LISTEN
- Be positive
- Don't be defensive

Be Willing to Take a Risk

One of the reasons given most often for not practicing collaborative decision making is that individuals fear failure. They do not have confidence in the members of the group to "do it right." They are unwilling to take a risk. A leader has to be convinced that *all of us are smarter than any one of us.* Accepting this concept will allow leaders to (1) give decision-making groups all information and support that they need and (2) trust that the process will produce decisions that will be good for the Community Learning Center. Will those decisions be the *right* decisions every time? The answer is no. But, it is important to learn from mistakes and take action to fix the problem.

The key to success is to make sure that collaborative decision-making group has all the available data and trust that need so that they will make the best possible decision. And when those decisions prove to be wrong, the group must be committed to studying the results to see how to make it better the next time around. This is the definition of a learning community that is willing to practice continuous improvement. Over time, the quality of the decision making will improve as members of decision-making groups get better at using information and data to make sound decisions, and as they also get better at working as a team.

References

Mohr, N., & Dichter, A. (2001, June). Building a learning community. *Phi Delta Kappan, 82*(10):745.

Prince William County Public Schools, http://www.pwcs.edu/admin/qmp.pdf.

National Center for Community Education (2000). *21st century visioning:*

The planning process workbook. Available online at www.nccenet.org.

Webster, W. E. (1994). *Voices in the hall: High school principals at work* Bloomington, IA: Phi Delta Kappa Educational Foundation.

Walters, K. E., Caplan, J. G, & McElvain, C. K. (2000). *Beyond the bell: A toolkit for creating effective after-school programs.* Oak Brook, IL: North Central Regional Educational Laboratory.

Winters, R. (2001, May 21). Pulling in the parents. *Time Magazine,* (p. 76).

10

Community Education Foundations

Journey into Community

Community Education is the philosophy that drives everything we do in the Community Learning Center. Our community members know that they can look to the center as a place where they might go to find resources to meet their educational and social needs. The community also knows that the facilities of the center are available for their use when they are not needed for instruction and extracurricular activities for the students enrolled there.

People feel a sense of ownership that is missing in many traditional schools. They talk about *our* Community Learning Center, even if they don't have any children attending classes there. They are willing to contribute the time and talents that they have to making a difference in the education of all members of the community, from preschool age to senior age.

Community Education is the energy that creates the movement toward a renewed sense of community that must exist in order for people to come together to make their communities better places to live.

Today's Community Learning Centers are part of an evolution that began back in the 1930s in Flint, Michigan. Frank Manley, a physical education instructor in the Flint Public Schools, was interested in developing recreation and educational programs that would keep kids in school and reduce juvenile delinquency. He teamed up with Charles Stewart Mott, a local wealthy industrialist who was a good audience for Manley's ideas. Mr. Mott was interested in starting a Boy's Club in Flint. Manley quickly pointed out that the schools could be used as a meeting place for a Boy's Club.

Mr. Mott provided $6,000 for the first experiment with using schools in Flint as community centers. The first experiment resulted in droves of citizens coming to the school when the doors were opened at night. After a full accounting of what was accomplished, Mr. Mott provided another $10,000 for visiting teachers,

> to go into the homes of so-called delinquents to find out what their homes were like. They learned that you can't just give a kids a ball and a bat and expect him to do well in school if he has severe health problems, or if his mother is entertaining men and he is under orders to stay out of the house until 3 A.M., or if his parents are drunk. The schools started what eventually became one of the strongest adult education programs in the country. They brought parents together in groups to talk over their problems and develop a sense of belonging." (Edwards, 2002, p. 25)

After those early experiments with opening up the schools, Frank Manley made an observation that later turned out to be the very foundation of today's Community Learning Center.

> We found that everything is so interrelated, physical health, mental health, education, the curriculum, the teaching, the family, the everyday living, and so on, so that you can't pull them apart and say that any one segment is going to take care of these social ills. So I thought the best chance we have is if we brought all these forces together. ... As soon as

you get one community started and they begin to
believe in each other and have a better understanding, then you can spread that out in a little wider
circle. ... (Appeared in Edwards, 2002, p. 26)

As Edwards observed, "The community school vision was
clearly Frank Manley's, and the provider was clearly, C. S.
Mott" (p. 26). From that point on, the Manley–Mott partnership led to the development of the Community School model
that was to be replicated in communities across the country.
Over the years the Mott Foundation has provided millions of
dollars in support of Community Education. It has provided
training for leaders, seed money for schools wanting to become model Community Schools, and support for a national
movement.

Community Education Defined

As a graduate student, I had the privilege of working
with one of my mentors, Dr. Maurice Seay, on a book titled, *Community Education: A Developing Concept*. In the
first chapter Seay presented a definition of Community
Education that seems to have endured over the ages and
offers help in understanding the concept today. Seay
wrote, "Community education is the process that
achieves a balance and a use of all institutional forces in
the education of the people—all of the people—of the
community" (Seay & Associates, 1974, p. 11).

Bumps in the Road

The movement was not without some bumps in the road.
In some communities Community Education came to be
known as the "evening program." It was identified with programs like adult education, recreation, and community development, with little connection to what went on in classrooms
during the day. The concept of Community Schools seemed to
only begin at 3:30 in the afternoon when the students were
dismissed from classes.

When budgets got tight, school boards were quick to scrutinize funding for Community Education. It was often viewed a luxury that was expendable in tough times. The U.S. government got in the act in the 1970s, when the Community Schools Act of 1977 was passed. That act provided funds for the development of model Community Schools in all the states. Then in a federal budget crunch, that funding was rolled into an omnibus education bill, and that was the last federal dollar to support Community Education for the next 25 years.

Community Learning Centers Legislation

During the administration of President Bill Clinton, Secretary of Education Richard Riley and Assistant Secretary Terry Peterson led the effort for the passage of a piece of landmark legislation, the 21st Century Community Learning Centers Act (Public Law 103–382 [H.R. 6]). The administration proposed that public schools become Community Learning Centers. In 1996, President Clinton eloquently outlined the vision for the future of schools:

> Increasingly, our schools are critical to bringing our communities together. We want them to serve the public not just during school hours but after hours: to function as vital community centers; places for recreation and learning; positive places where children can be when they can't be at home and school is no long going on; gathering places for young people and adults alike. Bringing our schools into the 21st century is a national challenge that deserves a national commitment. (William Jefferson Clinton, President of the United States, July 11, 1996; Retrieved, September 19, 1997 at http://www.ed.gov/pubs/ LearningCenters/execsum. html)

Congress then moved to identify key components to define the Community Learning Center as they wrote the legislation.

- A local public school serves as a center for the delivery of education and human services for *all* [emphasis added] members of the community.

- Public schools should collaborate with other public and nonprofit agencies and organizations, local businesses, educational entities, recreational, cultural, and other community and human service entities for the purpose of meeting the needs of and expanding the opportunities available to the residents of the community served by the schools.

- By using school facilities, equipment, and resources, communities can promote a more efficient use of public education facilities.

- The high technology global economy of the 21st century will require lifelong learning to keep America's workforce competitive and successful, and local public schools should provide centers for lifelong learning and educational opportunities for individuals of *all* [emphasis added] ages.

- The 21st Century Community Learning Centers enable the entire community to develop an educational strategy that addresses the educational needs of *all* [emphasis added] members of local communities.[1]

Political Compromise

The effort it takes to obtain congressional support for a new initiative is monumental. Each political party has its own agenda and its own view about the role that the federal government should play in the arena of education.

---

1   FN 1 U.S. Code Annotated, Title 20, Education, Chapter 70,
·   Strengthening and Improvement of Elementary and Secondary Schools, Subchapter X—Programs of National Significance, Part 1—21st Century Community Learning Centers.

The need for political compromise has led us to the point where we find ourselves now, with funding for Community Learning Centers limited, for the most part, to support for afterschool programs for children. Hardly anyone along the political spectrum could argue with the need to provide safe places for children to be after school hours. The concern shared by many Community Educators is that we run the risk of sending the message that all it takes for a school to become a Community Learning Center is to add an afterschool program (Parson, 1999).

There is a challenge that must be faced if the promising vision of the Community Learning Center is to be realized. That challenge is for communities to examine the concept of the Community Learning Center and to decide which components would work best for them. They can then explore ways to find the resources needed to transform their schools into Community Learning Centers. They may be surprised to find that many of the components of the Community Learning Center are either already in place, or could be put in place without the expenditure of great resources.

The Future

The future is bright for the Community Education movement and Community Learning Centers. As some of the early grantees of the 21st Century Community Learning Center Act have reached the end of their grant funding, they have found ways to sustain their efforts. Many of them have found that one key to sustainability has been extending the model for their Community Learning Center to become inclusive of many of the components proposed in the original legislation, including quality afterschool programs. They are making facilities available for community use when they are not needed for classroom activities. They are helping to address the lifelong learning needs of the whole community. They are collaborating and partnering with agencies, organizations, and businesses to make good use of the resources of the community. And, they are involving the members of their community in a collaborative decision-making process to create high lev-

els of ownership among people who used to feel distant and
alienated from their schools.

Progress is ongoing and gaining momentum at every turn,
in spite of tough economic conditions, threats of terrorism and
the realities of war, and challenges to our values as a nation.
We are seeing citizens band together to strengthen their communities with Community Learning Center as a centerpiece
for this movement.

No Child Left Behind

The administration of President George W. Bush sent
shock waves through the education community with the passage of the No Child Left Behind (NCLB) legislation. Among
the many features of that legislation, there are a few that are of
particular interest to Community Educators. First, the 21st
Century Community Learning Centers program remains a
part of total education package. A major difference is that the
administration of the program has been shifted from the federal government to the state. Localities now apply directly for
funds from their state education agencies, and decisions about
who receives funding are made by the state.

In the past, the grantees of the 21st Century Community
Learning Center program had to be local education agencies
(school districts). Community-based organizations (CBOs)
could participate, as partners with schools, but the funds had
to flow through the schools. Under the new legislation, the
funds can go directly to CBOs, and they are responsible for
working closely with their local schools.

Another focus of NCLB is on accountability for student academic achievement. States are required to put in place standardized tests that measure the academic progress of every
student, in every school. Within that system of accountability
is a provision for the identification of "failing schools," in
which parents are allowed to remove their children and enroll
them in another school where students are making acceptable
academic progress.

The provisions in NCLB for mandating parent and family
involvement in the planning and decision making that goes
on in the schools carries some major implications for Commu-

nity Educators. If ever there was a time when school districts need the skills that Community Educators have in building collaborative relationships in the community, that time is now. A plan for involving parents, families, and communities in the schools will need to be developed. Community Educators are well positioned and well prepared to provide leadership to these planning efforts.

Research Support for Community Education

The research base for Community Education has been thin from the very beginning of the movement. To address this issue, the Coalition for Community Schools recently released a report that contains a synthesis of evaluations that have been conducted on 20 Community School initiatives throughout the United States.

The report (Blank, Melaville, & Shah, 2003, p. 40), *Making the Difference: Research and Practice in Community Schools,* found that "[75] percent of the evaluated initiatives achieved improvement in individual academic achievement—results that speak to the power of creating environments and opportunities in the school and community that satisfy all the conditions for learning."

Fourteen of the evaluations examined the whole-school environment. The evaluations cited in the study show significant improvement in parent engagement as well as increased staff support for providing child and family support. (p. 42). A sample of results reported by some of the other studies showed that in Community Schools there was an increase in student attendance, reduced discipline problems, increased access to physical and mental health services, and greater contact with supportive adults. Although the sample of studies is small and the data are limited, readers are encouraged to access the full report on the Coalition's website (http://www.communityschools.org).

A Worldwide Movement

Those of us who live in the North America sometimes become very insular in our knowledge of what is going on in other parts of the world. A few will venture outside the borders to see what is going on, but sadly, we often think we are the only ones doing what we do. In the field of Community Education, there is much to be learned from some of the communities around the world that are making great strides in developing Community Learning Centers.

There is a remarkable man named Csaba Lorinczi who is referred to by some as the "Godfather of Community Education" in Eastern Europe. He recently shared a statement that he found on the wall of a small village community center in Bihor County in Romania. Translated from Romanian, it reads:

> There are lot of small people
>
> Living in lot of small places
>
> Doing lot of small things
>
> [Who] can change the world

There are indeed a lot of small people all over the world doing small things to make their communities and the quality of education better. They may call it different things, they may organize it and fund it in different ways, but when you look closely it all shares a common Community Education foundation.

Lorinczi also shared the definition that is used by the Community Education Project he works with in Central and Eastern Europe:

> Community Education is a structured way to assist people to improve their lives through education, culture and recreation, as learning is a lifelong process. The schools can provide the human and material resources to deliver these services via Community Schools. (Csaba Lorinczi, private communication, April 22, 2003)

Compare that with the simple definition of Community Education, as practiced in Robbinsdale, Minnesota, and you can see the similarities.

> Our goals are simply put: To connect schools to community, community to schools and create a learning community where everyone, not just children, are participants in learning, not just a spectator. (Bob Whitman, private communication, April 22, 2003)

In the Australian Capital Territory near Canberra, the Council of Parents and Citizens Associations published a paper titled, "School and Community Links: Objectives and Priorities." That paper addressed their vision of the Community School.

> Community schools extend the concept of public education beyond the traditional K–12 program. At the heart of the community school concept is a simple idea: Schools are not just places to teach children, but learning centres for the entire community because learning is lifelong. They also serve as a "hub" for a range of community-based services. They provide key facilities in their communities. (ACT Council of Parents & Citizens Associations, 2000, p. 2)

The paper went on to comment on the basic idea that learning and other aspects of family and community life are interdependent and impact on each other: "The learning of young people takes place within a whole community of adults and other young people. It can be enhanced or hindered by what is happening in other spheres of family and community life" (ACT Council of Parents & Citizens Associations, 2000, p. 3).

When we look closer to home at our neighbors to the North in Saskatchewan, Canada, we can find another definition of Community Education that fits well with what we have examined from other parts of the world.

Community Education is a philosophy based on community involvement and lifelong learning. It is a belief that schools alone cannot do all that is needed to help children and youth achieve success in their lives. Community Education promotes the interrelationship between the school and the family, and the school and the community. (http://www.sasked.gov.sk.ca/k/pecs/ce/whatiscomme d.htm)

In West Wales in the United Kingdom, we find a concern for rural schools becoming centers for their communities. Battling for the survival of their school, members of the Moylegrove community stated that:

Rural Schools have a history of vulnerability. We can now see a future in which their strength is forged, by extending beyond their traditional role, making use of their position at the heart of the community, to become a resource that supports and maintains a vibrant rural society. (www.villages-need-their-schools.co.uk)

The Network

A support system for Community Education has evolved as the movement has grown. There is the National Community Education Association (NCEA), a membership organization with headquarters in Fairfax, Virginia. The organization has a history of over a quarter of a century of service to Community Educators and Community Schools. They are also becoming a voice on Capital Hill when it comes to education legislation in the United States. NCEA is also the home for the International Community Education Association (ICEA). ICEA provides a place for the exchange of ideas about Community Education from communities around the world.

The National Center for Community Education was established by the Mott Foundation to serve as a place where people could come to learn more about Community Education. Thousands of people have traveled to Flint, Michigan, to participate in training programs at the center.

With the passage of the Community Learning Centers legislation, William White, President of the Mott Foundation, pledged initial support of $50 million to a unique partnership with the U.S. Department of Education. The funds were to provide training and support to the hundreds of teams that were the leadership of the 21st Century Community Learning Center projects funded by grants from the U.S. Department of Education. The Mott Foundation turned to the National Center for Community Education to organize and deliver training in locations across the country. After more than six years of existence, the Mott Foundation's commitment to the partnership has grown to a figure approaching $150 million.

The National Center recruited a team of two dozen trainers from different backgrounds and different locations. This team has designed and conducted training programs for 21st Century Community Learning Center staff and community partners on a regional basis, involving thousands of participants.

With the support of these and other organizations in the network, Community Education can continue to grow in the years ahead. It will take some bold leadership at the national, state, and community level, but that leadership is emerging all around us. The future for Community Education and Community Learning Centers is as bright as it ever had been.

Every day you can pick up a newspaper and read about a school or a school district implementing a new "reform" strategy that is closely aligned with the Community Education philosophy. This represents a process of movement from what we have come to expect from traditional schools to schools that are more and more becoming Community Learning Centers.

References

21st Century Community Learning Centers Act. U.S. Code. Vol. 20, secs. 8241 et seq. (1994). Lexis-Nexis.

ACT Council of Parents & Citizens Associations (2000). *Community schools the way of the future.* (http://www.school parents.canberra.net.au/community_schools.htm).

Blank, M., Melaville, A., & Shah, B. (2003). *Making a difference: Research and practice in community schools.* Washington, DC: Coalition for Community Schools.

Clinton, W.J. (1996). "Visions for the future of schools." Retrieved September 19, 1997 from http://www.ed.gov/pubs/learningcenters/execsum.html.

Edwards, P. (2002). *Frank Manley and the community school vision.* In Decker, L. (Ed.), *The evolution of the community school concept.* Boca Raton, FL: Florida Atlantic University.

Parson, S. R. (1999/2000, Winter, pp. 9–11). After-school programs: A beginning, not an end! *Community Education Journal, XXVII*(1 & 2).

Saskatchewan Department of Learning. (2003). "what is community education?" Retrieved August 8, 2003 at heep://www.sasked.gov.sk.ca/k/pecs/cc/whatis commed.htm.

Seay, M. F., & Associates. (1974). *Community education: A developing concept.* Midland, MI: Pendell Publishing Company.

Resources to Support Community Learning Centers

The following organizations and agencies represent excellent resources to support the development of Community Learning Centers.

Organizations

America's Promise: The Alliance for Youth

> 909 North Washington Street
> Alexandria, VA 22314-1556
> (800) 365-0153
> www.americaspromise.org
>
> *Resources to support developing a community network to support the needs of children & youth.*

Boys and Girls Clubs of America

> 1230 West Peachtree Street, NW
> Atlanta, GA 30209
> (404) 815-5765
> www.bgca.org
>
> *Programs and services to promote & enhance the development of boys and girls.*

Boy Scouts of America

> 1325 West Walnut Hill Lane
> Box 152079, Irving, TX 75015-2079
> (972) 580-2000
> www.scouting.org
>
> *Youth development program resource.*

Charles Stewart Mott Foundation

> 1200 Mott Foundation Building
> Flint, MI 48502
> (810) 238-5651
> www.mott.org
>
> *Grants to ensure that community education serves as a
> pathway out of poverty.*

Center for Community Partnerships

> University of Pennsylvania
> 3440 Market Street, Suite 440
> Philadelphia, PA 19104
> (215) 898-0240
> www.upenn.edu/ccp
>
> *Provides a model for university partnerships with com-
> munity schools.*

Center on School, Family & Community Partnerships

> Johns Hopkins University
> 3003 N. Charles St. Suite 200
> Baltimore, MD 21218
> (410) 516-8800
> www.csos.jhu.edu/p2000/center.htm
>
> *Research and technical assistance on developing part-
> nerships with families.*

Children's Aid Society

> 105 E. 22nd Street
> New York, NY 10010
> (212) 949-4917
> www.childrensaidsociety.org
>
> *Excellent manual, "Building a Community School,"
> available for free download.*

Children's Defense Fund

25 E Street, NW
New York, NY 10010
(202) 628-8787
www.childrensdefense.org

Source of data on issues affecting our nation's children.

Coalition for Community Schools Institute
for Educational Leadership

1001 Connecticut Avenue, Suite 310
Washington, DC 20036
www.communityschools.org

Source of publications on Community Schools.

Communities in Schools, Inc.

1199 North Fairfax Street, Suite 300
Alexandria, VA 22314
(703) 519-8999
www.cisnet.org

Model programs for creating partnerships with communities.

Cross Cities Campaign for Urban School Reform

407 South Dearborn Street, Suite 1500
Chicago, IL 60605
(312) 322-4880
www.crosscity.org

Source of information about community-based school reform.

Families and Work Institute

330 Seventh Avenue
New York, NY 10001
(212) 465-0244
www.familiesandwork.org

Research providing data to support community development.

Family Resource Coalition of America

> 20 North Wacker Drive, Suite 1100
> Chicago, IL 60606
> (312) 338-0900
> www.frca.org

Resources to strengthen and support families.

Fight Crime: Invest in Kids

> 1334 G Street, NW
> Washington, DC 20005-3107
> www.fightcrime.org

Resources for school and south violence prevention planning.

Girl Scouts of the U.S.A.

> 420 Fifth Avenue
> New York, NY 10018-2702
> (800) 247-8319
> www.girlscouts.org

Resource for youth development programs for girls.

Institute for Responsive Education, Northeastern University

> 50 Nightingale Hall
> Boston, MA 02115
> (617) 373-2595
> www.responsiveeducation.org

Resources for connecting school, family, and community.

Institute for Education and Social Policy

> 726 Broadway
> New York, NY 10003
> (212) 998-5880
> www.nyu.edu/iesp

Resources to help strengthen urban schools.

Learn and Serve America Corporation for National Service

> 1201 New York Avenue, NW
> Washington, DC 20525
> (202) 606-5000
> www.cns.gov
>
> *Resources for developing service learning.*

National Center for Community Education

> 1017 Avon Street
> Flint, MI 48503
> (800) 811-1105
> www.nccenet.org
>
> *Training and technical assistance for community education.*

National 4-H Council

> 7100 Connecticut Avenue
> Chevy Chase, MD 20815
> (301) 961-2808
> www.fourhcouncil.edu
>
> *Program resources for youth development.*

National Association of Elementary School Principals

> 1615 Duke Street
> Alexandria, VA 22314-3483
> (703) 684-3345
> www.naesp.org
>
> *Resources for afterschool programs & service learning.*

National community Education association

> 3929 Old Lee Highway, Suite 91-A
> (703) 359-8973
> www.ncea.com
>
> *Resources for training technical assistance and program development.*

National Institute on Out-of-School Time

> Wellesley College
> Wellesley, MA 03282-8259
> (781) 283-2547
> www.wellesley.edu/WCW/CRW/SAC
>
> *Resources for developing high quality afterschool programs.*

School-Age Notes

> P.O. Box 40205
> Nashville, TN 37205
> (615) 242-8464
> www.schoolagenotes.com
>
> *Technical assistance and training for afterschool programs.*

Schools of the 21st Century
Bush Center in Child Development and Social Policy

> Yale University
> 310 Prospect Street
> New Haven, CT 06511
> (303) 432-9944
> www.yale.edu/bushcenter/21C
>
> *Community school model that incorporates childcare and family support services into schools.*

Search Institute

> 700 South Third Street, Suite 210
> Minneapolis, MN 55415-1138
> (612) 376-8955
> www.search-institute.org
>
> *Resources for character building programs for youth.*

Southwest Education Development Lab

> 211 East 7th Street
> Austin, TX 78701-3201
> www.sedl.org

Resources for involving families in student learning.

U.S. Department of Education

www.ed.gov/21stcclc/

Resource for developing and operating a Community Learning Center.